There was a Time...

Childhood Memories of Manchester and Salford

Ken Loran

Edited by
Cliff Hayes

PRINTWISE PUBLICATIONS LIMITED

© Printwise Publications Ltd. 1991

Published 1991 by Printwise Publications Ltd
47 Bradshaw Road, Tottington, Bury, Lancs, BL8 3PW.

Warehouse and Orders
40-42 Willan Industrial Estate, Vere Street,
(off Eccles New Road),
Salford, M5 2GR.
Tel: 061-745 9168
Fax: 061-737 1755

ISBN No. 1 872226 10 8

Edited by

Cliff Hayes

Printed & bound by Manchester Free Press,
Paragon Mill, Jersey Street, Manchester M4 6FP.
Tel: 061-236 8822.

Many of the chapters in this book first appeared in Northern editions of

The Daily Telegraph

and are reproduced by kind permission.

There was a time
that I can recall,
a woman in clogs
wrapped up in a shawl

Reproduced by kind permission of the artist Harold Riley.

INTRODUCTION

It was during what we journalists call the 'silly season' that I first started writing the chapters which form this book. As Northern Editor I was editing a supplement for the Northern editions of The Daily Telegraph entitled 'Looks North' which was a compilation of 'off the diary' subjects with a 'North only' flavour. I wrote the first chapter and, feeling that it would be presumptive of me to run a series of similar type articles without a second opinion, asked the powers that be in our London office what they thought. They liked it and so 'I remember' which later became 'Memories' came into being.

I had a fund of stories about early childhood in the 30s and 40s to relate and it very soon became obvious that I had struck a chord with Northern readers. The letters started to pour in with people telling me how they, too, remembered similar incidents from their childhood. Repeatedly the question was asked 'When will you make a book of the articles? I hadn't thought along such lines but repeated requests led me to believe that such a collection would be well received. It has taken two years to re-edit, re-write in some cases, and get the timing right for the launch of such a volume.

I will always be grateful to the readers of Northern editions of The Daily Telegraph for urging me to go ahead with this project. I hope they, and newcomers to the articles, will enjoy the outcome.

KEN LORAN
NOV. 1991

Harold Riley

Harold Riley, the internationally famous artist, has been a close friend of the author for many years and has contributed several photographs and drawings for this volume. It is his drawing on the cover which inspired the title. Harold Riley still lives in his native Salford. He was a pupil of L.S. Lowry and the two artists collaborated on several works. Harold Riley was a pupil at the SLADE and became famous for his Salford paintings which he now considers his life's work. His portraits have included three Popes, members of the British Royal Family, three Presidents of the United States and many famous people. In recent years he has involved himself with sporting subjects, mainly golf and Association Football.

ACKNOWLEDGEMENTS

The photographs on pages 14, 52, 66 and 68 have
been reproduced by kind permission from
''Chimney Pot Park'' by Harold Riley.

Extra photos and postcard lent by Ted Gray and
Chris Makepeace, local historian.

Many of the chapters in this book first appeared in Northern editions of

The Daily Telegraph

and are reproduced by kind permission.

DEDICATION

For my dear wife Margaret

and remembering a life-long friend, Denis
Hinchliffe, whose companionship helped to make
many of these chapters possible.

CONTENTS

Chapter One

The Day War Broke Out

Like Rob Wilton — and just as in modern times in the case of the death of President Kennedy — I remember exactly what I was doing 'the day war broke out'. We were (although my contribution at age seven was minimal) building an air raid shelter to be shared by four families. I remember work stopping and everyone bending an ear to open windows to hear Chamberlain announcing that "No such undertaking having been received... etc". It meant little to me at the time but I learnt later of the terrific impact on the adults. Stoicism prevailed (British phlegm you know) and after the announcement (and the necessary cuppa) everyone got on with the building of the shelter.

Now my father was a man who read little, slept a lot and worked hard. He was also a master of do-it-yourself before the phrase was ever thought of. It was nothing in our household to see him fill in one doorway in the kitchen and knock through another one to suit my mother's whim, only for her to change her mind again and want the original doorway restoring. He did all that without a murmer — in fact I think he enjoyed the challenge — it takes all sorts. He even tried to pass on his expertise to me — with no response at all. Even to this day I still have some of his tools languishing in the garden shed — they may be worth a bob or two but they don't get used much. Get a man in is my motto.

Anyway, father was i.c. shelter building. Do you know that shelter was part of our lives for a total of ten years? It was built so sturdily we couldn't demolish it until the timbers started to rot. Hitler had no chance!

The main body of the kirk was comprised of railway sleepers which never, in all the later years when the place became gang headquarters and storeroom for the garden furniture and lawnmower, lost the smell of creosote. The roof, sides and floors were all made of sleepers. Who got them and from where I never did find out. Then we had the seats. These were all double 'courting couple' affairs from the local 'flea pit' cinema which was updating its image. They had had a lot of use and weren't the freshest smelling seats around but it was wartime and they served their purpose. We had a pail lavatory and two exits/entrances — and most of the structure was in our garden.

Where we lived was on top of a hill overlooking Trafford Park — then one of Germany's prime targets because of its war production — and very close the recently opened East Lancashire Road. The folk-lore of the time was that in the light of the moon the East Lancashire Road glistened and was easily mistaken by German bombers for the Manchester Ship Canal which ran alongside Trafford Park. I always felt there was an element of truth in that because we got more than our fair share of bombs considering the town was really only able to offer the mills and the odd pit. Definitely not strategic.

I remember sneaking out occasionally to watch the fires over Trafford Park from the top of our hill and see the bombers getting caught in the searchlights. (Very impressive to an eight year old). One very strong memory of those days was of hearing what we all thought was a bomb whistling overhead only to find out next morning that it was the bacon slicer from the nearby grocery stores flying across two streets to land — harmlessly thankfully — in someone's garden.

That shop was totally destroyed apart from the wall holding up the staircase under which the family were sheltering. They survived without a scratch while all around them was totally destroyed. It transpired that the grocer had used his adjoining garage for all his stock. That, too, stayed intact although every tin and package in the place was 'blown' by the blast and rendered useless.

It wasn't useless to our gang though. We were admonished not to eat anything but were allowed to play with the jams and fruits and rice etc that filled the place. Heaven! The garage became our meeting place for weeks to come until the smell became unbearable. It was there that the gang became an entity. Then it was back to my father's wonderful shelter.

I remember going to the ice cream van in our street in Harpurhey in Manchester in the early 30s and saying: "I don't want one like this" (holding my two palms together) "I want one like this", (holding my hand in a fist). I was four and, of course, I wanted a cornet and not a wafer. The ice cream man got the message.

I remember a time during the war when my grandmother and I were caught in the middle of Manchester during one of the regular air raids.

We went into the basement of a warehouse on High Street along with a lot of other unfortunates. The raid lasted for ages (or so it seemed to my young mind) and I distinctly remember an elderly man getting up from our bench and wandering off into the darkness. Soon the sound of water falling could be heard and I remember my grandmother turning to an elderly lady alongside and with a sour expression muttering: "He couldn't wait." Can you imagine how she would feel if she saw some of the drunken antics of today's youngsters.

I remember the Christmas blitz in Manchester — the famous one that is. My father and mother had been to visit my grandmother in Harpurhey — we lived in Swinton at the time, a long journey in those days — and because of the air raids had had to stay overnight. I remember the bombs dropping as we sat in the shelter just off Windsor Road and neighbours seemingly constantly running in in tears shouting — "They've bombed me house" — "Someone's trapped in number 14" — "The dog's been killed at number 23" — "Has anyone seen me mam?" And so it went on. We survived that night — although how I don't know because the 'shelter' was just a pile of old timbers with a roof which sat about three feet above surface of the street. The ground was so hard it was impossible for the menfolk to dig the trench any deeper.

I remember the next morning us setting off for home. We managed to catch a trolley bus on Conran Street and that got us to High Street in the centre of Manchester but that was the end of public transport for the day. It seemed as though the whole of Manchester city centre was ablaze. We emerged from High Street into Market Street and looked briefly at the burning warehouses in

Piccadilly — a sight that will live with me forever — and then made our way down Market Street towards Salford Bus Station which was just below the Manchester Cathedral. As we got nearer we saw Exchange Station ablaze from end to end. Sparks were flying everywhere and as it was Christmas my mother had put on all her finery, including an imitation fur coat. My father and I spent our whole time brushing sparks off the coat as we got nearer and nearer to the bus station. Our efforts were not very rewarding for the coat — when we eventually examined it in the safety of our home six miles outside Manchester — it was pretty well ruined. We walked those six miles home and all the way we saw tired firemen in side streets beside their machines resting after the trials of the previous night. Smoke and sparks were everywhere and to my small mind, it was exciting, though also frightening. It was not a brave face that emerged from time to time from the shelter of the inside of my father's overcoat where I hid from the falling debris.

I remember, too, my first encounter with children of my own age when we moved from the slums of Manchester to the relative salubriousness of an estate in Swinton — then just being

Manchester Blitz at night.

My first picture.

developed as suburb. It was an old mill and mining town which was being taken over by incomers from the Manchester slums who were trying to better themselves by buying — at about £350 — or renting houses. Most of them at that time — in Swinton at least — seemed to be built by the Lanes Brothers. They were as different as chalk and cheese those two. One tall and arrogant and the other small and plump who drove a Jaguar car and seemingly had to sit on a cushion to see over the top of the steering wheel.

Anyway this little lad knocked on our kitchen door on our first day in the new house and my mother answered. Inquisitive me — though reticent — was peering from behind her. "Does your lad want to join my gang?" said the little lad. "Who's in it?", asked my mother. "Me" he said. I joined.

I remember how that gang grew into a regular group of around six who got into all the scrapes and troubles kids of that age do — especially growing up during wartime.

Let me tell you more about that gang — who stayed together throughout schooldays from the age of six and seven to 14 and 15. It was augmented — when the mood took us — by other temporary members who had a passing use — such as good golf ball hunters (more about that later), good stickleback catchers from the railway embankment streams (they never seemed to last more than a couple of days before they floated belly up to my intense disappointment), or had mothers who were not stingy with the home made toffee and home made lemonade. Do you remember those fluff encrusted toffees, by the way, which were produced grudgingly from the depths of some intimidated child's pocket.

Chapter Two

The 30 Year Shelter

I said I would return to some of my father's do-it-yourself exploits, his shelter which would have outlasted a 30 years war. The garage he built actually did last over 30 years.

The shelter went at last when he decided to buy a car. But the decision to buy a car meant some major demolition and construction work so it was a long time before it actually appeared.

This was in the late 40s when I think even father was convinced there wouldn't be another outbreak of hostilities. So the shelter went — inwards. He dropped the roof, dropped the sides onto that and was left with a back garden considerably higher than when we first moved in.

That was stage one. Stage two necessitated building a double sized path at the front. That meant the removal of about three dozen roses. That done he then had to knock down his beloved shed and store his tools in the spare room until the garage was built.

Stage three was the demolition and re-erection of a huge coal bunker round the back of the house. That meant miserable trots for a shovel-full of coal in the pouring rain, instead of a quick dive across the path from the side door.

Stage four was the building of the garage itself. This was put right at the back of the garden on the raised bit where the shelter had been. That meant having a ramp — that was his undoing.

The car arrived. He drove it proudly into the garage (or nearly) and hit the sump on the top of the ramp.

Now because of various tricky path and house configurations, it was not possible to stretch the ramp so father decided to drop the floor of the garage by about 18 inches. That sounds easy, doesn't it? Try it sometime. How many cubic feet of concrete and rubble had to be moved I hate to think. All I know is that I was the labourer with the wheel-barrow who had to shift it 200 yards each load to a piece of spare ground.

Anyway it was done bit by bit with a concrete wall being created on which the garage eventually rested. It took weeks. I went back to the road in which we lived some 30 years later and the garage — which was only a wood and asbestos affair — was still there. I don't think the owners could knock it down and anyway it might even have become a listed building by then!

He built cupboards that were better built than the house and always seemed to be decorating.

Talking about decorating I remember I was always press ganged into stripping off the old wallpaper — a heck of a job in those days — but was never allowed to touch one wall in the dining room. Years later I found out why. One of the original painters had painted in huge letters, 'Joe gone for a .... be back in five minutes'. Despite his d-i-y skills father could never get that off the wall.

It's funny how people change. It was nice being brought up in a household where father could do just about anything from woodwork to shoe repairing and would never dream of getting someone else to do his decorating whereas I — certainly in recent years — have not followed his teachings and, if a job needs doing around the house, say 'Get a man in'.

I remember my father always seemed to be DOING something and if he wasn't busily occupied then he would fall asleep in his chair. There never seemed to be an 'in between' period or, if there was, I don't remember it.

He took two years — with able help from yours truly — to point the brickwork of our house, the painting of the house inside and out took on something of a Forth Bridge aspect — as soon as you thought he had finished he started again.

He loved working with wood and scorned wriggly nails to join the pieces. The joints had to be properly fashioned and 'made to last'. I think anyone who could destroy a piece of my father's handiwork would have deserved a medal!

There were no half measures about shoe repairs either. Out would come his last and his pieces of leather and nails and he would sit on the living room floor repairing all the family footwear. I think he learned shoe repairing skills from a professional he knew — an old school friend called Brogan whose father had fled the family home leaving Brogan to support his mother and brothers and sisters.

Virtually every Friday night a rather tipsy Brogan would arrive at our house and go through the same routine. He would sit in the middle of the floor and empty his pockets of his week's takings — minus, of course, what he had spent in the pub. He would then divide the money into three piles

Those lovely footbridges where we could lean out and let the steam of the passing railway engines envelope us.

and as he did so he would say 'That's for my rent, that's for my leather, that's for my mother — and if I catch my bloody father I'll kill him'! The litany never changed.

Father would make cupboards that you would need one of those ball and chain contraptions to demolish, he was a dab hand at concreting. In fact he got so obsessed with his prowess at one time that he virtually concreted the entire back and front gardens. But he loved roses, entered shows and won prizes, so their needs stopped him just in time.

He was on first name terms with just about every workman in every timber yard, ironmongery and builders' merchants around and was regularly to be seen with a wheelbarrow full of sand or cement, bricks or chippings or with a bundle of planks on his shoulder and his pockets bulging with screws and nails.

He was an able bricklayer and erected many coalbunkers. He erected many because he always seemed to put them in the wrong place for my mother and have to demolish them and re-erect. He could 'wipe a joint' and many neighbours were glad of that skill in those days of frequent burst pipes in under-heated houses. He also had an allotment with, naturally, the best vegetables around growing there. He could mend watches, repair and even build bicycles but motor engines and the inner workings of cars and motor bikes totally baffled him.

He was a terrible photographer, couldn't play a note on any musical instrument and only ever seemed to read instruction manuals. He was a brilliant roller skater, though, and played roller hockey for Belle Vue and, with my mother, gave exhibitions of roller dancing at the early Butlin's holiday camps.

My father was called Cyril but hated it and throughout his youth was always known to his friends as 'Sid'. The story goes that when he was courting my mother she went one evening to the door of the dressing room at Belle Vue where my father was playing for the hockey team and asked if Cyril was nearly ready. Nobody knew a Cyril but closer questioning revealed Cyril's secret. He forgave her — but only just!

In all these activities I was always the apprentice. I learnt how to do all the things he could do, but never as well as he did them — hence my current philosophy — 'Get a man in'!

Proud Dad and me.

15

Chapter Three

Family Gathering

I want to really go back in time to a period I can vaguely remember and to some family anecdotes that were passed on to me.

I think my father and mother had ambitions to be nomads because in the seven years of my life before we moved to Swinton and I really started to be able to settle down to what passed in those days as a good childhood we lived in four houses — and I was not born in any of them!

Now that may sound a bit 'double-dutch' but this is what actually happened. At the time I was born we lived in a little terrace house in Cumberland Street in Lower Broughton. I was the first child born to any of my great grand-father's grandchildren (that almost sounds 'double-dutch as well) and he wanted it to be a 'safe' birth — so he insisted on the birth taking place in his rather grand house round the corner in Grosvenor Square — so that had to happen because great-grandfather held the family purse strings and had to be appeased.

Not long after THAT event we moved to Annis Street in Harpurhey and not long after THAT to Windsor Road in the same district of Manchester. Not long after THAT we moved to Downham Crescent in Prestwich near to Heaton Park and not long after THAT to Swinton and a rest at last!

I never knew my grandfathers. One was killed in the First World War and the other (on my father's side) died a week before I was born. I had two lovely grandmothers, though, who spoiled

Sitting precariously, and certainly not comfortably, on the gatepost at No. 8 Grosvenor Square, Lower Broughton.

me rotten, and a great grandmother and greatgrandfather — old Rip Rap the family used to call him.

Old Rip Rap had been quite prosperous at one time having a plumbing contractors business just off Chapel Street in Salford but he had fallen on hard times when a builder in North Wales went bankrupt owing him a lot of money. He soldiered on for some years before eventually retiring and letting his daughters look after him — shades of Hobson's Choice there I can tell you.

The family was very close knit with lots and lots and 'aunts and uncles' always ready to give me a 'three-penny joey' if I stood at the door as they left. If you had a lot of 'aunts and uncles' as I had that soon mounted up at weekends.

It was the custom for all the family that could to meet at great-grandfather's house on a Saturday evening after everybody had dashed round Smithfield Market in Manchester just as it was closing to get to 'sell-off' bargains from the market traders. You know I can still remember the naptha flares on the stalls and that lovely market smell of vegetables, toffee apples and cloth. We always started with a walk down Tib Street where all the pet shops were. Those little dogs (riddled with distemper my father always used to say) looked so longingly at passers-by that few could resist them.I know over the years, distemper or not, father bought me about three — and he was right - distemper saw them all off.

We trapmed down to Greengate to get a tram to Lower Broughton. The family would slowly gather and it was also a custom that the adults played cards (usually Newmarket) while singing hymns. Great-grandfather would sit by the fire smoking his clay pipe and at each refilling put a 'dottle' from a previous smoke on the top of the new tobacco.

Great-grandfather would always say at about 10-O-clock 'Well I like your company but I don't like your hours' and off he would go to bed. Although he would say the same thing every week

as soon as he was through the door the room would burst into laughter with my rather round Aunt Cissie unable to laugh like everyone else but indulging in a fit of 'tee-hees' in a corner.

On one memorable night while this was going on great grandfather re-appeared in his Scrooge nightgown and cap. He'd forgotten his beloved pipe and had walked across the room for it before the group saw he was there — probably because of the tears in their eyes. 'Silly lot of buggers', he remarked and stalked off. The laughter after that was uncontrollable and I'm told my Uncle Jim ruptured himself through laughing and had to go to hospital!

Me and Aunt Cissie who was renowned for her 'tee hee' laugh.

With my long suffering great grandmother — the one who used to cheat at patience!

I distinctly remember my great-grandmother — in fact I have a picture (it's on the cover) of her looking long suffering with me as I am crying my eyes out about having to have my photograph taken. She was bed-ridden most of the time I knew her but I remember paying visits to her bedside. She came from a huge family from Preston and had, I think, thirteen brothers and sisters. She had a picture of them all at the foot of the bed and I used to delight in asking her to tell me their names.

Like a child doing his 'tables' she would recite - 'There's our Sarah, our Liz, our Jim our John our Fred etc etc. Oh I can hear her now.

Another thing she used to do was play interminable games of patience. She had a bed in a downstairs room and the family would gather across the hall. Every so often the old dear would cheat to make a game 'come out' but when she did everyone knew because she couldn't resist whistling as she did it!

During those long hours playing Newmarket I used to hang around behind the players and if anyone need to go to the lavatory I would 'take their hand' until they came back. Oh joy and oh even more joy if I won the odd couple of pence for the player — we only played for a penny a game one on the face card 'horse' and one in the kitty. Those games used to get hectic as home time neared and 'horses' were removed from the centre so that more and more money was put on the remaining card or cards. It was an unwritten rule, too, that anyone having 'leads' to the cards had to 'dump' them which they dutifully did. It's a wonder anyone ever got home from those games.

Then it was the late bus home and I can remember on the nights it rained sheltering under my father's long raincoat and peeping out at the passers by and imagining they didn't know I was there. A bit like the ostrich I suppose but you never think about little legs sticking out when the rest of you is hidden.

I remember that house of my great-grandfather's so well — or some of it. It had cellars with the door at the end of a dark hallway full of hanging coats. As a small child that was a terrifying place and I wouldn't go near it. I remember if I wanted to go to the lavatory on the first floor running like mad up the stairs, bolting the bathroom door and then waiting until I thought the 'coast was clear' before diving back down the stairs and emerging among the card players breathless. I did go down the cellar via the back yard during daylight but somehow never thought of it as being the same place as the one at the bottom of that passageway! The house also had attics but I never ever went up there - that was asking far too much particularly as one of my uncles used to regularly regale the family with tales of the ghosts he had seen up there. Someone else also said they had seen a ghost 'slide up the door of the outside lavatory in the yard' — I never went in there either hence my panic stricken forays up the stairs.

I remember my parents telling me about an 'understanding' my great grandfather had with the local cinemas.

It seems that every Monday great-grandmother would leave her husband his evening meal and go off to the cinema. When he had finished he would join her. They had the same seats every week (no one would dare try to sit in them) and great grandfather paid when he arrived with great-grandmother going through 'on the nod'. Each week they alternated cinemas between the Victoria and the Tower which were both on Great Clowes Street in Lower Broughton.

It transpired that this particular night great-grandmother got her 'fixtures' wrong and went to the Tower while great-grandfather went to the Victoria. Nobody noticed that they were in the wrong cinemas in the dark and both sat there in splendid isolation until the interval. It was too late by then to rectify the situation (and anyway who would lose face by admitting they got it wrong) so it seems they both decided to stay where they were. A small incident but one which cropped up repeatedly whenever the family got together.

Great-grandmother died when I was quite young but I remember being taken in to the front room to see her in her coffin. It was the first dead body I had ever seen. Great-grandfather lasted for some years but became incontinent and a burden to his children who were themselves getting on by that time. When he died the family gatherings started to become less frequent and finally tailed off altogether. I have not seen some members of the family for many years living as I do in the great underbelly of Manchester — Cheshire. A pity really.

Another common occurence was for me to leave home about every other Saturday when I could not get my own way about something.

This usually happened in the Windsor Road house in Harpurhey. I would take umbrage about something and stalk out with my little attache case packed with all my worldly treasures. Remember I was only about six or seven at the time. I was always a strong willed child.

Now little known to me I used to often wear an old chauffeur's cap on these journeys (my father's brother had been a chauffeur among a myriad of other jobs he had in his lifetime and had handed this piece of redundant equipment on to me) and the peak of the cap would appear before I did as a would peer round the corner of a side street to see if anyone was taking notice of my momentous decision to leave. No one ever did of course and only later did I realise the great mirth my exploits caused. Needless to say I always seemed to relent and forgive everyone when meal times approached!

On Great Clowes St. there used to be an army barracks — Lancashire Fusiliers I think — and in those days there was a lot of patriotic bugle blowing and drum banging going on. At the first hint of this I was out of the house and standing on the corner of Cumberland St to watch the troops go by. I always managed to sneak a few hundred yards further up the road after the band had gone and press my nose up against the window of the local toy shop — I remember it was called Gilberts and it was full of Dinky Toys and lead soldiers. I could rarely afford to buy anything but oh! the delights spread out before a young child in that shop.

And there were the trips to Belle Vue. I still have family pictures of me with a huge giraffe in the background and others with the floral clock. I have little recollection of those events — but I know I was there — I have the pictures to prove it!

What a mecca Belle Vue was in its heyday. A zoo, fairgrounds, speedway, dog racing, exhibition halls — a full day out and right on the edge of the city. When I became a father I used to take my children to Belle Vue at Christmas to see the circus. They were about the same age as I was in the photographs. I wonder if they remember that. Belle Vue has gone now. Houses stand where the entertainments once were.

I remember that like so many other Manchester families Blackpool was our holiday treat. I can also remember that we stayed in back street 'digs' and that I used to howl the place down if I couldn't see the sea and the sand. If I couldn't see them as far as I was concerned I wasn't in Blackpool and that was an end of it. I used to scream 'I want to go to Blackpool' within about 20 yards of the sea

With mum and a young friend at the Floral Clock in Belle Vue pleasure gardens.

front! I must have been a real pain in those days.

We went to North Wales a lot, too. I can remember one occasion during the war when we were due to go to Deganwy. My father had injured his hand just before the war and could not 'join up'. He did his bit in the Ford factory in Trafford Park, though, and also became a special constable. But he felt deeply his inability to take part in the fighting.

On this particular occasion we were to catch a train from Exchange Station to Llandudno Junction and then change for Deganwy. I can remember now the station announcers of those days — rather prim they were — The train now standing at platform two is the 2-30 for Chester, Rhyl, Prestatyn, Abergele, Old Colwyn, Colwyn Bay and Llandudno Junction. Even in those days they were very precise and pronounced it properly as 'Clandidno'.

Anyway we had to walk alongside what used to be called the longest platform in Europe — it linked Victoria and Exchange stations and was so long it changed its number several times. On this occasion it was lined with hospital trains bringing injured soldiers back from the fighting. All the doors were wide open and I remember to this day the racks of 'Tommies' either three or four deep on stretchers in the wagons waiting to be moved.

We walked a little way along looking as those poor fellows and after a while my father turned round and said: 'We're not going. I can't go away after seeing that.' We didn't go either and I remember it was only after the war that we ever went on holiday again.

But the holidays we did have throw up a mass of memories. I remember sitting in the balcony of the Winter Gardens with my grandmothwer watching my aunt (my father's sister) dancing with a woman friend on the floor below. She was only young and had married just as war broke out. Her husband was away in Egypt with the RAF and she would never dance with another 'chap'. Not many could make that boast in those days — particularly when the Yanks came.

We would go on the Pleasure Beach. I went passed it in the late '80's and while a lot has changed drastically some things seem to be constant. The first thing we would make a bee-line for was Noah's Ark and that was still there. Next would be the Fun House and the Laughing Clown and finally (when the money was getting low from too much candy floss and waffles) there would be just time for two final rides on the Chair-o-planes and the Grand National (I always rated that better that the Big Dipper) and then it would be back to the 'digs' for the evening meal. Gosh we had simple tastes and needs in those days, but we did enjoy ourselves.

A trip up the Tower and a visit to Madame Tussauds were always on the week's agenda and a trip to Bispham on the trams was a must. Oh! those trams. They still have that haunting 'toot' (or some still do) and every time I hear it I remember happy childhood days in Blackpool.

What a shame it has all to end and we gravitate to pints of lager and kiss me quick hats. Still I suppose those people get their pleasures in simple way too so who am I to knock it?

Chapter Four

Bogies, Skates and Dens

Let me set the scene for you of the place where I spent much of my childhood.

It was a modern estate — a mixture of private and rented houses (yes people could actually rent privately in the 30s and 40s). The main road on which I lived linked the old Manchester Road and the new East Lancashire Road and off it were several 'drives' — we'd progressed from common streets. The main road was flat for most of its length but dropped sharply down to the East Lancashire Road.

Most of the area opposite my house was taken up with an old 'open air school' for the sickly of the area and its new replacement. For all the time I spent in that house — right up to getting married — that field was the main focal point of my childhood.

It was a child's delight. Collapsing wooden buildings which nobody did anything about, except the children of the neighbourhood who had ready made building materials for the 'dens' that sprouted up all over the place, and masses of old cobbles for building barricades for our 'war games'

Slowly as we burnt and demolished most of the structures we found we had cleared an area sufficient for us to play both cricket and soccer and this we did interminably. I can well remember games lasting from about 9-00 in the morning until 8-00 at night with scores like 154-80 and the members of the teams changing constantly as meals were taken, home work done and errands run.

I remember one lad in our gang whose mother had a very penetrating voice. He lived two 'avenues' away from the scene of soccer combat but she could be heard across the rooftops with a shout of 'Briiiiiian' at meal times. Brian used to pretend he hadn't heard her (although I'm sure most of the rest of the town did) and played on. Then his younger sister would be sent to fetch him — also to be ignored and finally the mother herself would appear. He went then with a clout behind the ear each time. I suppose he thought it was worth it.

We built dens and then 'bombed' them with the owners still inside. Great lumps of masonry were used and it was common for the sides of the dens — usually built out of cobble stones about eight high with a corrugated iron roof — to collapse on the occupants. I can never remember anyone getting seriously hurt (they say God looks after drunks and kids) although such actions were usually followed by a bout of fisticuffs.

Talking about corrugated iron reminds me of some dry sledging I indulged in once. In the field where we normally staged our winter Olympics on sledges in the snow — Bamber's Field it was called — we once tried dry sledging using corrugated irons sheets as the sledges. I remember my hitting a rock half way down while going at a rate of knots, being hurtled forward

Barton Road, Swinton in later years. No. 53, where I spent much of my childhood, is the one with the car outside on the road.

only for the 'sledge', having bounced off the rock, coming back and pinching my behind between it and the rock. I had a weal for days after that!

Now that hill I was talking about was great for 'bogies' — those contraptions made out of old pram wheels and lengths of timber. Some were elaborate and some quite primitive — it depended whether your dad had had a hand in the making I think — but they went like the wind down that hill. I remember once Brian failing to turn at the bottom of the hill and hurtling right across the East

Lancashire Road and onto Swinton Golf Course. Nothing hit him as there was very little traffic in those days. I bet he couldn't make it half way across now before being pulped.

Our other form of transport were roller skates extended to about a size 16 foot. The seat was formed by the biggest bumper annual you could either lay your hands on or sacrifice (it had to be at least three years old for that sacrifice to be made) and all you did was stick your legs out and steer with your weight. Great fun with the bravest going three avenues down before turning off as the East Lancs Road loomed but most of us risking only one or two. Inevitably we fell off as we tried to take the turn — but what were a few more grazed knees among friends — we always seemed to have grazed knees.

I thought I would make a 'bogie' recently for my grandchildren but as someone told me, 'you can't get the wheels, you know'. He was absolutely right. In those days it was a pair of high coach built pram wheels for the back and two trolley wheels for the front. Nowadays you can only get the wheels off folding prams etc and they are absolutely useless for your true bogie.

But our prize means of transport were bikes. Not everyone had one though and the child who had one would often find it hard to resist the bribes offered to 'give us a ride on yer bike'. I remember my first one. It was home made. I scrounged an old black frame, stripped it down and (great luxury) walked down to Broad Street in Pendleton where there was a shop that would stove enamel

frames. They wouldn't let you on the bus with bike frames so I walked there one week and brought it back on foot the next (I only found out having got there that they only stove enamelled once a week).

Next I had to save up or scrounge for the rest of the parts and build the thing up slowly. Obviously I got a lot of help from my father but when it was finished it was MINE and all the more precious for having been hand-made. I still had that bike when I first started work and the only alteration I made in that time was to put a pair of 'drop handlebars' on it. It seemed more in keeping for a teenager trying to impress.

I hope readers will forgive me jumping around in time and not keeping to a chronological pattern but as I sit in front of this computer keyboard memories suddenly flood back and you feel compelled to get them down as quickly as possible.

I remember the wartime 'Stay at Home' holidays. Not much of a holiday really. All the Government did was send us a concert party which travelled from town to town for about three days in each place. They kept pretty well to the old 'wakes week' dates that the mill towns used to have before, and for some time after, the war.

I remember one year when it was Swinton's turn we had a concert party in Victoria Park. I went to the first day and was totally smitten by the young girl who sang 'Oh Johnny, Oh Johnny, how you can love'. I was very impressionable at that age (I was seven when war broke out) and would have followed that young singer to the ends of the earth. The concert was performed every afternoon for three days. I was there ogling at every performance always getting as near to the bandstand as possible.

After three days she went out of my life for ever but I never forgot her and only recently I was telling a dear friend of mine, Jill Summers who plays Phyllis in Coronation Street, about my smitten childhood. "That was my sister", she said. Small world isn't it.

Funny how things remain in memory. I can remember the first film I ever saw — it was at the Rialto (a bingo hall now I suppose) and it was Rose Marie starring Nelson Eddy and Jeanette MacDonald. I remember it so well because for years afterwards (and still now) I recall the scene where the little boy is about to pull the whistle on the crane which will blow the whole thing up.

I remember going to the Adelphi Cinema on three consecutive nights with my grandmother in an attempt to see Gone With the Wind. I had already seen it at the Gaumont in Manchester with my father and mother, having had to queue for about four hours for the privilege. Anyway when it finished its Manchester run the suburbs got a chance — nothing has changed — and off I went on a Monday night with my grandmother.

Just as the old coloured retainer was knocking on the door to bring news to Scarlett O'Hara a notice flashed on the screen to the effect that an air-raid was in progress and would 'patrons leave the cinema'. (They said things in that style in those days — the days of bobbing white ball over the words for community singing).

Now it was the custom and practice at the Adelphi that if the show was interrupted by air raids you got free admission the next night. How they ever made any money during the height of the raids I'll never know.

Anyway next night back we came. At exactly the same moment — the knock on the door — the air raid warning appeared. We went back for a third try (the last night because the show changed mid-week) and at exactly the same moment the air raid signs appeared. It was only years later that i realised that it wasn't stretching coincidence to its limits that this happened. It was simply that the German raiders left their airfields at the same time each evening and thus arrived over Swinton at the same time each night. It felt weird at the time though and grandmother never did see the film.

We had a lot of cinemas around us in those days. I can remember the Adelphi, the Ellesmere (posh that one), the Plaza and the Palace (the traditional Northern 'bug hut'. There were others a decent walk away such as the Palace at Monton, the Ambassador at Pendleton and the Odeon at Prestwich. As kids we haunted them all, saw hundreds of films (two shows a week changing on Thursday and a different one, usually rubbish, on Sundays). As we got older we didn't much mind the rubbish on Sundays because by then we had cultivated an interest in girls and what the film was was a matter of little consequence.

I think as children the highlight of the week was the Saturday afternoon matinee. On reflection it was very low grade material that they dished out to us. But there were some good moments and anyway half the fun was trying to sneak in for nothing and, once in, (reluctantly usually having had to pay) sneaking under the seats to get to the highest priced ones. Little heads used to be popping up all over the placed all the time looking to see how far they had progressed.

We had the Three Stooges (when it was Curly, Larry and Moe, Shep hadn't appeared at that time) and we had Roy Rogers, Gene Autry, Tom Mix and Hopalong Cassidy (I remember his side-kick Andy Devine — he of the squeaky voice), the cartoons always got the best cheer of the afternoon (audience involvement was total) but the place used to go deadly quiet for Flash Gordon and his battles with the Emperor Ming.

The great thing when they let us out at 4.00 was to identify with the films we had just seen. Don't tell me that what you watch (i.e. violence of television) doesn't influence you. Even those seemingly innocent B westerns influenced my innocent compatriots.

We we would pour out and head for home with cries of ''I'm him on the white horse'', ''I'm the main man'', ''I'm Tom Mix'', etc, etc, all the time beating our backsides with our hands in a childlike imitation of spurring on our horses.

Reminiscing about the Saturday afternoon matinees when we watched Flash Gordon, Mickey Mouse, Buck Rogers and our other heroes. The only thing about those matinees we didn't enjoy were the love scenes when catcalls would drown out the dialogue and lads would curl up and hide their faces asking their friends to tell them, when the 'slutchy' bits were over. The only other time the catcalls were heard was when the film broke. I have often wondered since how those operators managed to think let alone rewind the reel with so many youthful voices in full catcall.

But those were the early days. Later when we started to ponder seriously about girls we didn't even think about buying cheap seats. It HAD to be the back row and NOT just the back row of the stalls but the back row of the circle. Ice cream and, occasionally, a bar for fruit and nut chocolate had to be provided (for someone really special you pulled out all the stops and bought a bar of Caley's Milk Tray, not a box, a bar with six different pieces in each bar). There was absolutely no question of going 'dutch' the lad paid and that was an end of it.

Those visits had to be hard won because money was tight and I suppose that resulted in some premature, mostly frustrated, fondling and fumbling in an effort to get some return for the outlay. In most cases it was a waste of effort and perhaps the only thing to come out of it was the cultivation of a vivid imagination as you described the events of the night before to your friends. On such tellings are reputations destroyed.

Nowadays if you go to the cinema it's difficult to know which has the X certificate — the goings on on the screen or the goings on around you and I do mean around and not just on the back rows.

In the 40s and 50s when cinema attendances were booming and cinemas seemed to be on every street corner we in Swinton had at least six within easy walking distance and girls knew how they stood in your estimation by which cinema you took them to. After all 1s 9d (old money) for the back row of one cinema was only 1s 6d at another and that was important to financially straitened lads.

Everyone of those cinemas had two shows a night and changed the programmes on Thursday with a special low budget film on Sunday evenings. I think they used to show the low budget stuff on Sunday because they knew they had a captive young audience with all the youth clubs

East Lancashire Road, 1934-39.

and other sources of entertainment closed.

One cinema I recall, the Olympia at Irlams o' th' Height changed its bill three times a week plus the Sunday show. As I say if you could afford it you could watch pretty well endlessly — rather like the television programmes of today.

In another cinema, the Princess at Monton near Eccles, they used to have 'love seats' — twin seats without an arm rest in the middle — on the back few rows. Obviously they were in great demand and booking was essential.

As I say the fumblings were not only surreptitious and often futile but they had to be carried out with care because the usherettes seemed to be patrolling constantly with torches zooming in on miscreants and they used to also have a nasty habit of standing behind the back rows and shining their torches on couples when things started to get too heated.

Mostly we went to 'first house' shows because we had to be in bed before the second showing was over. I remember coming out of the first house on Saturday evenings and being able to buy the Sunday Empire News containing the afternoon's football results. That has reminded me of the intense interest there used to be in football 'pinks' 'greens' and 'buffs' (that was the Bolton paper) each publisher using a different colour of newsprint for these special editions.

I suppose it was the lack of television for instant reportage that gave those papers their heyday. We used to listen to the litany on the radio 'Manchester City 2 Liverpool Nil, Manchester United 4 Oldham 1...etc' and then wait eagerly for the cry of 'Football Special' as little newsboys ran rapidly around the streets selling the words of wisdom from soccer writers who had actually BEEN to the match and were telling us blow by blow how those results were accomplished. There doesn't seem to be the interest in football specials now. If you want one you go to the corner shop. Blame television.

In later years I used to do an afternoon shift on the Evening Chronicle in Manchester as a sub-editor and I handled many of those reports. Doing that soon destroyed any illusions one might have had about deathless prose. The sub-editor would be allocated about six matches and he would treat them as 'running' stories receiving about 40 words every 20 minutes from each reporter. It was rather like keeping balls in the air as a juggler trying to remember which particular piece went with which particular earlier piece. You also had to write a headline after having only received the first half report. You can imagine the frustration of writing 'City in the driving seat' when the final result was City 2 Arsenal 4 or 'United on Top' when the final result was United 2 Notts Forest 3. You soon learnt to play safe. Believe me writing headlines for that type of report is quite an art.

But back to the cinema. When I was 'courting' my wife-to-be had a very strict father and his rule was that she had to be in by 10 p.m. First house was out because we both worked and couldn't get there early enough so we used to walk out, usually at the most critical part of the film, so that she could be home in time. It was only when television came on the scene that we finally managed to see the endings of all those films! I wouldn't mind but her father would then keep her up until all hours telling her how bad it was for her to be out late!

Some years ago Harold Riley, the celebrated

Northern artist, and good friend had a birthday party. What did he do? He invited all his friends to the Palace at Monton near Eccles and showed us the whole of the Flash Gordon episodes in one sitting. You can't beat that for a birthday celebration!

Money was vitally important as we got older and started 'courting'. I can distinctly remember telling a girl I would see her 'inside' (the cinema that is) simple because I didn't have enough money to buy her a ticket. I wonder how many potential love affairs were destroyed because lads of my time had to resort to such tactics.

Sunday evenings were the time when trysts that would last (for about a week usually) were made. I recall the Ellesmere cinema was the scene of much of the posturing the 'young blades' indulged in at that time.

The Ellesmere had a wide central aisle that split the cheap seats from the dearer ones — not that many youngsters used the dearer ones. The routine was to wait until the interval between the shorts and the main film when the lights went up and walk, nonchalantly, but obviously, to the 'gents' in the sure knowledge that the girls would see you. Those visits to the toilets took an age as lads would wait for others to join them and compare notes about who was in the cinema and what the 'prospects' were.

Endless messages were passed by intermediaries about who was prepared to 'go out' with who and where meetings would be made later. It was common for someone to ask another if they had 'clicked' yet — meaning had they made a date with a girl.

We used to have a 'bunny run' on Sunday nights — that was the only night it counted as a 'bunny

Cheeky me with Dad on the tandem which we took all over the North West — including the Mersey Tunnel.

run'- when the boys would walk up one side of Chorley Road and the girls down the other. At the Market Place and Town Hall the directions were reversed. Various messages (and catcalls) were passed by willing, sniggering, messengers and, amazingly, the right boys got with the right girls for however long the relationship lasted — usually not very long.

Our focal point was a place called the 'Stingo' a temperance cafe where you would get hot vimto and root beer served by a Mr Towers who had remarkably prominent eyes which seemed to bore into you like a gimlet, He ran a tight ship did Mr Towers and if you weren't buying then you couldn't stay in the warmth of his establishment for very long.

But relationships were forged in that place and on the 'bunny run' which, in some cases, lasted for a lifetime. I still recall friends who met their future wives in those circumstances and despite the pressures of modern living they are still together.

Notes were also sent from hand to hand across classrooms with cryptic messages saying 'Will you go out with me tonight'. By the time they had been read by everyone along the chain and it reached the recipient (sometimes it was intercepted and destroyed by a rival along the way) it had gone through so many hands that it was not at all clear who had originated the note and it was far too dangerous to just nod in the affirmative in case you thought it came from the wrong girl and you ended up with a 'tug' to the endless delight of your mates,

Jumping forwards a little I remember my friend Denis and I were courting two girls from Stretford and we lived in Swinton. That meant a journey of about six miles and being 'strapped for funds' most of the time we used my father's tandem as our main means of transport to meet the girls. Our journey used to take us through Trafford Park and necessitated complicated arrangements about where we would meet up later. Thankfully in those days it was safe to leave things in fairly public places and we used to leave the tandem and then rendezvous later at the 'parking spot'.

I recall on one occasion cycling through Trafford Park which at that time was littered with railway lines set into the roadway. We got stuck in one of the tracks, keeled over with the tandem wheels bending to form a perfect right angle. Try walking six miles in step with a tandem on your shoulders!

So that was 'courting'. Meeting girls — via intermediaries ('My friend wants to know if you fancy him'?) in odd places. Avoiding meeting them where your friends could see the encounter and ridicule you, using the plentiful youth clubs and cinemas but always, always, saying 'I'll see you inside'. Hard times but innocent times with only a hint of lust.

This was the bike I made with help from my father. The 'drop' handlebars were a must. I was 14 and had just started work when this was taken.

Chapter Five

Those Monday Mornings

When we moved to Swinton to the modern estate, the school we were all to go to, wasn't finished and so we were scattered all over the place.

I was sent to St Stephens, a Church of England school near the Market Place. Even in those days it was a historic building and looked about ready for the bulldozer (in fact it was used for many years after). Do you know that even in 1939 they were using slates and slate pencils! We had morning assembly and then were divided by sliding partitions into three classes. The partitions were supposed to cut out the noise from the other classrooms but they didn't and you would be writing on your slates doing elementary 'sums' while at the same time listening to the geography lesson next door one way and about the Norman invasion on the other. How we ever learnt anything is a mystery — not that we learnt a lot there anyway.

I remember the lavatories were at the bottom of the yard and to a little lad in a hurry that yard seemed like a mile long. There were 'accidents', of course, and I remember twice having to escort a rather smelly classmate home after he had failed to make it down the yard. Of course mothers were always home in those days and the 'disaster area' was soon cleared up and sent back for further lessons.

We had our music lessons in the cellar I remember and I always longed to be allowed to play the drums or cymbals. Sadly I always got the triangle — do you remember those things — one note every eight bars (or so it seemed).

Anyway I didn't stay long at St Stephens as I graduated to the junior school ranks and as our school still wasn't ready I was sent to St. Peters which was right in the middle of town and, for us youngsters, a very long way from home. These days they'd probably lay on a special bus — we had to do it by Shanks's pony.

I remember little about that school except that it was totally alien and big and I never seemed to identify with it. I remember we seemed to have a lot of religious services in the adjoining parish church and that the playground was so big you could hide from the 'big 'uns' and not get set upon. I didn't stay there for long, though, because at long last our own school was finished and we moved yet again.

What a treat! A new school, new teachers (all of them women except the head) and it was right on our doorstep.

The building was flat-roofed and so was like a honeypot to little lads. Every evening (and certainly every weekend) we would hang around waiting for the caretaker to lock up and leave and as soon as he was out of sight over the wall we went and it was playtime all over again only this time it was illegal — and thus much more exciting.

So that brings me to a very strong memory. Monday mornings. Because always some nosey parker of a neighbour would report us for playing in the air raid shelters, on the roof or in the schoolyard and every Monday morning there would be the gang of five waiting nervously outside the headmaster's room for the inevitable punishment.

Our headmaster didn't use the cane. He used a plimsoll (they call them trainers now, I think).

Guilty as charged was always the verdict because in modern parlance we were caught 'bang to rights' and hadn't a leg to stand on. We hadn't a bottom to sit on after the retribution either because six of the best with a plimsoll was not very comforting.

We did the same thing week after week, though. Obviously the sinful pleasure far outweighed the sore backsides.

And they did because what child can resist sliding down the coke and through the coke hole into the boiler house and thus have a warm den in the evenings, out of sight of parents. Who can resist slyly opening a classroom window during the day and leaving it 'on the latch' so that you can push it open in the evening, get into one classroom and then lift the central heating panel and crawl through to every other classroom via the service 'tunnel'. We weren't vandals though. We didn't do any damage — we just enjoyed the vicarious thrill of it all.

But nosey neighbours didn't like our games on the roof (particularly when we took our bikes up as well and went from one level to another by way of rickety planks) and so every Monday morning the gang got their 'cummuppance'. We were notorious and (I think) got no little pleasure from that notoriety. We were the 'hard men' and didn't we love showing off to the girls?

But there were good times at the school as well.

We 'dug for victory'. Every spare bit of ground was dug up to grow vegetables and each class was allocated a plot. I remember 'trenching' for potatoes. Don't forget we were 'townies' translated into the suburbs as (I suppose) were the teachers and everything had to be done 'by the book'. We did grow some great vegetables but where they went I never did find out. Certainly they didn't appear as school dinners!

The school had two playgrounds. One was flat and was great for the fifty-a-side football matches with a tennis ball that the lads used to indulge in and the other was a steep sloping affair which was no good for anything — except in winter! Then it came into its own as a sliders paradise and the lads were eternally grateful that male chauvanism ruled.

Mr Kearns deemed it dangerous for the girls to have the sloping playground when it was icy and so (although the boys and girls alternated every week normally) come the ice and snow and the boys had the bottom playground. And to add to the delights the headmaster would instruct the caretaker that bucketsful of water should be poured down it whenever frost was forecast so that next day a highly lethal, but highly delightful, ice run was available for the boys. There were rules too. Nobody in wellingtons was allowed on it because that caused 'chucking' and nobody with metal studs in their boots could use it because that scored the surface.

Now this headmaster, Mr Kearns, wore purple suits (regarded by our parents with some degree of suspicion in those days of corduroy trousers and plain tweed jackets). On reflection I suppose he was what would now be called 'trendy' or 'progressive'. Whatever title we enjoyed what he did for us.

For a start there were the Friday afternoon film shows he arranged. He had his own 'magic lantern' type projector and would entertain us with scratchy old Charlie Chaplin comedies interspersed with 'worthy' documentaries for our last 'lesson' of the week. The whole school joined in these showings, even the infants, and Charlie Chaplin must have had a special magic because even if they could not understand the plot they could understand a pie in the face and laughed as loudly as anyone else.

Mr. Kearns allowed dancing lessons, that's where I learned the valeeta, the palais glide and the Lancers and I can distinctly remember us galloping around the hall arms linked and prancing like a group of carthorses to the sounds of 'Little Angeline'.

I only stayed at that school for the duration of three classes but they were enjoyable times.

Grosvenor Square, Lower Broughton, showing No. 8 (middle of picture) where Ken was born.

Although the headmaster gave the boys the icy treats (and the flexible plimsoll) he also insisted on integration in lessons. Even to this day I can knit (how many boys can admit to that and the rote of 'in, over, under, off' will stay with me forever. I can't do anything fancy but if you want a dishcloth then I'm your man!

We learnt to weave on miniature looms (I don't know if that would come as easy as knitting to me now).

I was too young to know but I imagine that he was something of a thorn in the flesh of the education authority for those were not the days when boys knitted, as we did, or schools indulged in mass weaving on miniature looms. And they were certainly not the days of organised cycle trips into the country with the headmaster at the fore. Whether they were or not Mr. Kearns indulged us in all these activities and I for one, will be eternally grateful for the chances his 'progressiveness' brought.

We had 'Old Tyme' dancing in the school hall on Saturday nights. I remember my parents dancing to the Cosmo Trio — one bald-headed drummer, a saxophonist and a pianist. Their range was limited but they were good and loud!. We kids would slide around on the dusted floor at half time making thorough nuisances of ourselves — showing off again you see!

But the real dances — the posh affairs with a real orchestra — were held irregularly at St Augustine's school when decorum was the order of the day and even at half time the kids had to remember their place and if any silliness was to be undertaken it had to be undertaken in the cloakroom. I learnt a lot of my dancing at those events either standing on the toes of a long suffering partner or practising secretly with another lad in the cloakroom. Goodness knows what we would have felt if one of the lasses had caught us doing it.

That reminds me of a friend of mine whose brother had ambitions towards a young lady but couldn't dance properly. The elder brother took him under his wing and for weeks showed him how to do the Moonlight Saunter. Came the big night and the younger brother set off to impress his lady love. He came back not long after fuming and saying: I'll kill you our Harry, I can't take'. The elder brother had taken the male role throughout the teaching and the pupil thus didn't know how to 'take' the lead. I suppose forgiveness for the humiliation came eventually!

Another of our 'head's' innovations, the one day cycle trips in the school holidays must have taken some organising but he always managed to get a good sized group together to make the journeys. I recall that as top class juniors we were in the proud position of either leading the way with Mr Kearns or actiing as 'whippers in' and encouraging the stragglers, a task that got increasingly difficult as the miles piled up.

We went to far away places from Swinton like Alderley Edge, Lymm, Dunham Massey and Styal. In these days of motorways and fast cars all those places are within about half an hour of Swinton. Then it was a full day on a bike there and back with pop and sandwiches at mid-day and countless stops while punctures were mended.

Those destinations were magical to town kids. It was real 'country' with cows and sheep not just cart horses grazing on a bit of spare grass, It was a chance to 'capture' strange creatures in matchboxes — we were always putting living things (usually cabbage white caterpillars from the allotments) in matchboxes with holes punched in the top. There were dragon flies to pursue and gaily coloured butterflies to fling your jacket at, previously unseen wild flowers to pick and take home to mum (usually the bunches were limp and beyond redemption by the time we got home).

There were rabbits to chase (vainly) and geese and ducks on the meres and lakes to admire and there were deer (you can still see them in Dunham Park) and there were the magnificent views to be absorbed from Alderley Edge. I remember there always seemed to be a pall of brown smoke hanging over Manchester to be seen from the Edge. I've not been back to check whether smoke abatement and Clean Air Acts have changed all that but I imagine they must have done.

Things were not all idyllic. I recall once being thrown into a bed of nettles by Mr Kerns for some misdemeanour although I can't for the life of me remember what it was I had done. For him to do something as drastic as that though it must have been pretty serious. And then there were the problems of keeping up. The tinies always lagged behind on the way home and, frankly, we 'senior juniors' were not that sure of the way home ourselves. However nobody ever went totally missing and the fact that I can fondly remember those trips even after all these years must prove that they were beneficial.

It's only later in life that we ever appreciate what people have done for us and how much of their actions and kindnesses have influenced us. I, and many more, will be forever grateful to Mr. Kearns for taking us 'townies' into the countryside and showing us that there was a better way.

Chapter Six

Poverty, Poverty Knocks

Will you come to my party, will you come
Bring your own bread and butter and a bun
'Cos my father's on the dole and my mother's
*   picking coal*
Will you come to my party, will you come

That haunting little ditty has been with me for many a year and I think it indicative of the hungry and hard 30s. It tells in a few lines of the hardship of the times, but it tells it with humour and it has reminded me of some of the hard times I can recall from that period.

I can remember being admonished when staying in Windsor Road, Harpurhey, not to go in certain houses because they 'had bugs'. I can also remember little lads showing me the bugs by lifting the pictures off the walls and watching the bugs scatter in all directions. I can also remember them showing me the bites they had received from the bugs. We were a 'clean' family and despite the close proximity of 'lousy' neighbours we never did get bugs.

I can also remember the gas lights we had in those days. Those delicate mantles were the bane of everybody's life and Lord help some heavy handed father of the house (perhaps on a Saturday night — it always seemed to happen then) who had had a 'few' at the pub and broke the mantle in his clumsy attempts to adjust the flame. Lord help the little lad who slammed the kitchen door and caused that delicate gossamer thing to disintegrate. Retribution was swift for such an offence.

If the mantles broke at the wrong time (was there ever a right time?), and, although you always had a spare it was not uncommon to break that as well they were so difficult to fix, then you had to either throw yourself at the mercy of a neighbour and beg to use their spare (not easy convincing them when it was also their only alternative source of light if they also were due to experience the clumsiness of a returning man of the house) or you endured the rest of the evening in candlelight. That put paid to most forms of entertainment, you couldn't read in that light, constantly being told it was 'bad for your eyes' and so until bedtime you resorted to sitting and watching the fire and conjuring up patterns and stories from the images thrown up by the flickering flames.

I have spent many an hour with my grandmother when the rest of the family were out on a Saturday night just watching the fire and listening to the big pendulum clock in the hall. Many's the time I have found myself in bed the next morning not knowing how I got there having been sent to sleep by that ponderous ticking.

But despite the shortage of money and the muck that abounded people did their best to keep 'decent'. There might be little behind them but the curtains were always clean, the steps donkey-stoned and the pavement brushed and, in the winter, kept clear of snow for the benefit of visitors and neighbours.

When you think about it now and read of the prices being paid for chamber pots (or guzunders — goes under the bed — as we called them) it's amazing. Every household in our area had several because every household had an outside toilet at the bottom of the yard — always as far from the back door as possible it seemed — and nobody, but nobody, ventured out there in the dead of night to answer a call of nature. The ritual was to take the 'guzunder' with you on the first 'call' of the morning -rather like prison slopping out I supopose.

It wasn't all perfect, of course, there were 'problem' families galore in those days as there are today but because of the strictures of the elders of the neighbourhood things were never allowed to get too far out of hand and a wife in trouble because her husband had drunk the week's money would always be able to borrow from others until next pay day.

People were always on the look out for ways of saving the odd copper. I can remember going with my grandmother to the gas works just off Rochdale Road — a walk of a few miles from Harpurhey — with a home made boxed truck to have it filled with coke. It was fractionally cheaper than having it delivered and so lots of people resorted to that way of getting fuel. I was too young and small to push that truck either full or empty but I vividly remember the trips.

I can also remember going to that same gas works for Saturday night dances, I was still a young child and there was nothing else the family could do but take me with them — pre-baby sitting days these. I would be made to sit on a chair at the side of the floor and watch the dancers without fidgetting! I was fascinated by the glass ball in the middle of the roof which would send shafts of multicoloured lights onto the dancers every so often. What a magical sight for a young child.

But talking of saving small amounts we had a trolley bus stop at the top of our road but it wasn't a 'fare stage' and so we never, ever, boarded a bus there. Instead we went to the next stop along and got on there. The number of times I have been dragged by running parents to catch a bus which suddenly took everybody by surprise by coming round the corner a minute early. You couldn't hear those trolley buses as could could ordinary buses and they did have a habit of creeping up on you! Coming back we did the same thing even in the rain and snow. I suppose I benefitted from the pennies that were saved by way of treats but I didn't appreciate it at the time.

We do tend to look back to childhood through rose coloured glasses and I suppose that is only natural. We DID seem to have endless long summer days when we were young, the winters WERE on time, WERE white at Christmas — in fact all the seasons behaved themselves.

But what of the discomforts. No central heating in those days. Who can remember the agonising cold of a winter's morning. The whole family either working or going to school so there was no time to light a fire before breakfast and in any case what was the point if everyone had to leave the house with no-one to enjoy the heat and also fuel was rationed.

Did you, as I did, sit in an icy cold kitchen fumbling with an already cold piece of toast and

marmalade and a cup of rapidly cooling tea before rushing upstairs for fling on your clothes and flee to the relative warmth of school.

And then coming home in the evening to an even colder house. First one home lit the already laid fire makings (Remember the shovel set upright resting on the grate with a piece of newspaper wrapped around it to make the fire 'draw'? No matter how carefully you watched it always seemed to burst into flames. And if you didn't wrap the burning paper up tight to cut out the flames it would fly up the chimney and set the soot on fire — then you really were in trouble!

By the time the evening fire was giving any warmth to the one room that was allowed to be heated the evening was over and it was time for bed.

Remembering things like that brings home the wonders of modern day living with central heating for most people and no shortage of coal and other fuels which was the order of the day during wartime — and, indeed, during post war shortages. Houses always seemed to reek of the smell of paraffin from secondary heating (the heaters always seemed to be black and made by Aladdin) and plumbers did a roaring trade mending burst pipes. Thank goodness my father was capable of 'wiping' the odd lead pipe joint or we would never have had running water during the severe weather.

As it was, if father couldn't mend the burst the water would have to be cut off and you couldn't have a fire in case the back boiler burst! Those paraffin heaters came into their own in those days as did 'night lights' those squat candles which would be put into a saucer with a little water in the bottom and lit and placed under the most vulnerable pipes. I wonder why builders delighted in putting the lead pipes on outside walls (usually facing north). Perhaps they had a deal with the local plumbers.

But there were good times as well. I remember the cold winter nights when my eyes would light up as father put on an extra shovelful of coal half-an-hour before our normal bedtimes. That meant only one thing.

In our house two of the bedroooms had minute fireplaces in them and it was the custom for father to put a shovel-full of hot embers into each 'grate' just before bedtime to (allegedly) warm up the room. The only thing those few embers did was to provide a lovely glow in the dark for a child such as myself as I lay there, curled up and slowly inching my feet into the icy depths of the bed as I gradually warmed the sheets up. It didn't seem quite so romantic at the time but in retrospect it seems a delightful experience.

And then there were the stone 'hot water bottles'. They were, indeed, made of stone but we didn't fill them with water. Instead we filled them with sand and put them in the 'bungalow range' oven a good while before bedtime to warm up — in fact to heat up to an unhandleable temperature.

Then a piece of old blanket would be wrapped round the 'bottle' and it would be placed at the top of the bed. When bedtime came the secret was to slide into the warm spot all curled up and slowly push the 'bottle' down the bed to warm the rest of it. I can never remember the bed being totally warm — I fell asleep before that happened, but I do have vague recollections of a surreptitious hand removing the bottle for use in another bed.

And then, still with cold winter days, there were the chapped legs. Nobody seemed capable of devising a way to keep up the stockings of young boys. They were of thick wool, slipped down your legs no matter what you did and in the cold you ended up with raw weals where the wellingtons rubbed against your flesh. Horrible that was and once you were afflicted it was the devil's own job to get the weals to heal.

I wore clogs at that time. I didn't have to but several of the children in my class did and so I thought I ought. The phase soon passed and I confess I can't remember much about clogs except for one winter when it snowed heavily (and of the right consistency) and we all were able to walk about one foot higher than normal because the snow clung to the 'irons' on the clogs and, if you were very careful, you could walk for a goodly distance before the packed snow fell from the bottom of the clogs and you were back to normal height again.

Our standard footwear was boots. Boots with lots of eyelets to lace up and, as I say, thick woollen stockings above them which always seemed to need to be pulled up about every ten yards. We tried elastic bands just below the knee but that was almost as painful as the wellington weals and so we always seemed to be resigned to having our socks round our ankles and having adults telling us to 'pull our socks up'. So that's where the phrase came from!

We had balaclavas — for the uninitiated knitted hoods with a gap at the front for the eyes, nose and mouth. They tended to get wet around the mouth area with too much talking on cold days and that was another ripe area for 'chapping' (lips this time) if you weren't careful.

Those, and pullovers — usually dark gray, but 'Fair Isle' for best, were the normal dress for young lads in those days with the addition, possibly, of a rather worn and baggy jacket. Not very sartorial, but it WAS the hungry 30s and wartime 40s — with rationing, so I suppose we had to do with what there was. I remember the jumble sales of cast off clothing were always popular.

Remember those pictures of the inmates of Belsen at the end of the war? Well every child I knew used to look like that when I was an infant and junior — shaved heads were the norm!

Everyone had what we called 'pudding basin' haircuts and the 'demon barbers' who perpetrated the crimes abounded.

My 'demon barber' was named Percy Flitcroft and he had a narrow back room behind a tobacconists in Manchester Road, Swinton just alongside the local "flea pit" cinema. It's strange to recall that, in these days of anti-smoking lobbies just about everyone smoked in those days and people could make a living just by selling cigarettes, cigars and, of course, snuff.

Anyway Percy had this primitive barber shop in the back room with just a hard bench for customers to sit on while they waited. You go to a 'hair-stylist' now and often you will be cosseted and pampered by a young lady who washes, trims and lotions your hair for an interminable time — at no small cost I might add. Not so with Percy. It was rather more like a production line in a car factory and as for smelly oils and lotions — there was no call for that sort of thing! Sixpence, no tip and away you went for another month.

He was no respecter of persons either, was Percy. It was not a case of "Could you move your head a little to the left, sir" with him. He grabbed it, pulled it into position and admonished you to keep it there until he was ready to grab it again and pull it into another pose. No wonder we called it having an 'all off' You could only stand the pain at infrequent intervals.

Still everyone was treated the same, even the adults, and everyone looked the same until it was time for the next torment, shaven headed with a cap that was suddenly a size too large. Wits would often come up to you after you emerged from Percy's and were walking home and say "Tell me who did it and I'll set the gang on him'- very droll.

But if Percy didn't see to you the 'nit nurse' would. 'Nit Nurse Nora' we used to call the school health visitor who would fumble around in our heads and proclaim us either 'nitty' or clean. With the big classes and the social deprivation there was then just about everyone had 'nits' and I can clearly remember the treatments — and humiliation. At home you would have to lean over the kitchen table with newspaper below you while your mother combed through your hair with a fine toothed comb laced in vinegar to get rid of the unwelcome visitors in your hair.

If one child in our school got an ailment you

could guarantee everyone did. Regular dosings with cod liver oil and malt and orange juice (during the war in little square sided bottles) and sulphur tablets were the order of the day with everyone keeping well clear of those who had had the sulphur tablet treatment for a decent interval!

I remember once being left in charge of the shopping while my mother went into yet another shop and, being totally bored, 'rooting' in the shopping basket, finding a bottle of syrup of figs and drinking the lot in one go. I won't go into the sordid details but readers who have experienced syrup of figs will know what the consequences were for me.

I suppose health visitors were very necessary in those days because washing was not the highest priority either for children or adults and clothing was worn for very much longer than it is today before being washed — it had to be given the performance that Monday morning washing days necessitated.

Lighting the fires in the evening on coming home from school or work was only half the story because for most of the week — and certainly in winter — you never really saw the fire. It was always surrounded by a 'maiden' loaded with washing which steamed everywhere out and caused constant dripping windows.

Those Monday morning wash-days were a ritual which could not be avoided. These days most households have washing machines and in some cases spin driers to help the job along. In my young days there were no such things. The Monday ritual was an all day performance from heating up the boiler, 'dollying' the washing in a tub and scrubbing it on a washboard to wringing it

My Grandmother and Mother at Scarborough.

out in a mangle — the blankets often needed two pairs of hands to get them through the rollers — and then putting it on the rack in the kitchen or on the maiden in the living room. You would get a glimpse of the flames through a gap in the wet washing and that was your lot!

Then there was the ironing. That also seemed to take days. No wonder we were always waiting for clean clothes, we didn't have enough and what we had was waiting to be "aired" — remember a shirt being pressed against a mirror to see if it was dry enough to wear — if it left a haze it was still damp and you couldn't wear it even if there was a young lady tapping her foot outside the cinema waiting for you!

Chapter Seven

Not All Innocence

They say that confession is good for the soul and I think I ought to tell readers that my childhood was not all innocence and long summer days. There were some times when I did and said things I regretted.

Like the time I was doing the 'my dad's better than your dad' type of routine with one of my friends and with supreme arrogance finished off with the riposte: 'Anyway at least we've bought our house and yours is only rented'. I got a bloody nose for that.

Then I was sitting with the gang on the bus when one of them was reading a new story in one of the comics — Adventure, Hotspur, Wizard, Rover, Champion — we shared them all between us at that time, 'swaps' were what made our world go around. Anyway this lad wasn't the brightest scholar in the world and he was laboriously reading this story out aloud. 'The new boy from Veenoos' he said. I turned round from the seat in front and said: 'It's the new boy from Venus you twerp' (we called people twerps in those days). I got another bloody nose for that one as well.

Then there was a fight in the school yard with a lad called Gordon. He was stronger than me and lay on top of me until I 'submitted'. I was sick after that because he smelt so much. I remember there wasn't a lot of washing either of clothes or person done by some people in those days.

Then there was a famous confrontatation with another lad who was two years older than I was.

At first I ran away from his bullying but father got to know about it and sent me out to confront the other lad. (Dad was no doubt watching behind the curtains to see justice was done). Anyway, surprise, surprise, I knocked spots off him — and in front of witnesses of my own age. I rose their estimation after that and the other lad was forever after called 'Skriker'.

Now this 'Skriker' was always leading us on to do stupid things. It was in the days of accumulators being charged every week to run the 'wireless' with lads carrying the delicate glass encased equipment to the local radio shop to be charged up. It was also the days of 'carbide' — pre Ever Ready battery days. Now carbide was used to power bicycle lamps and could be obtained in canisters from the local bike shop and we discovered that if it was poured into a milk or pop bottle and mixed with water and then the neck sealed with a bit of rag if you shook it vigourously and then threw it it would explode like a bomb.

We got quite adept at this and would have 'battles' throwing these carbide bombs and, as we did with fireworks later, seeing who could hold on longest before throwing the missile. On this occasion Skriker threw his bomb but nothing happened. We waited and waited and still it didn't go off. So Skriker walked over to find it in the long grass. He bent down — then it went off. He was scarred for life and we didn't play with carbide bombs after that.

But Skriker did other daft things. The front doors all had about fifteen small glass panels in them and he had a whippet which wanted to go out rather more often than Skriker was prepared to get out of the chair. He did no more than kick out one of the glass panels to give the dog free access. What his mother said I don't know (his father was away in the RAF) but the panel stayed out — much to the dog's delight.

He it was who decided we all had to become parachutists and scrounge bed sheets to make the parachutes. He it was who climbed our favourite sycamore and jumped off holding the four corners of the sheet. He it was who failed to realise he couldn't jump out far enough to clear the bottom branches and he it was who staggered off home full of scratches and bruises. None of us tried to emulate him after that exhibition.

Then there was the valley gang. Where we lived there was a railway cutting two fields away which separated our estate and the council estate. The cutting was a 'valley' as far as we were concerned and thus they were the' valley gang' and had to know their place. Any infiltrator into our territory was dealt with swiftly and we seemed to spend long hours in the playgrounds during the week arranging when and where to meet so that each side could seek retribution for some imagined slur.

It was nothing for lads to run home with bloodied heads from thrown stones and for one gang or the other to leave a captive strung upside down from a tree branch. When we ran off to compare how brave each of us had been and tell tales like fishermen about our deeds we always imagined the captive would be there all night. We never went back to look in case his friends lay in wait but our immature knot tying couldn't have been much good because nobody came to any harm.

We never did make peace with the valley gang. I wonder whether the children who live on those two estates today still have those battles?

At the bottom of that railway embankment there were two drainage channels which for some reason contained sticklebacks. We were allowed to 'fish' our side of the embankment and the valley gang 'fished' theirs. The problems arose when one side or the other infiltrated the other's territory. Always in those instances it was a case of 'Let battle commence'.

Those sticklebacks. I remember we used to take jam jars with string round the neck to bring them home in and then put them in glass fruit bowls (without permission I hasten to add). Funny how they always seemed to perish and be found belly up. We had a little more luck with larger fish and newts from the golf course ponds but they never lasted any length of time.

Talking of golf courses we could make the odd penny or two often by taking our clothes off and wading in to the pond to find a misdirected ball for a golfer — always in the right weather, of course — and made rather more by waiting until they were out of sight and THEN retrieving them to be sold at the club house door for much reduced rates.

Pennies went a long way in those days. I remember penny 'lucky bags' from the corner shop on the way to the Saturday afternoon cinema and favourites like Nuttalls Mintoes and Uncle Joes Mint Balls. Still going to this day and still as tasty. I also remember Walls's Snofruits. Whatever became of those — vastly different ot the modern ice lolly I can tell you.

And finally talking of pennies I must jump forward a little to 1944 when the war in Europe ended. The word went round on the children's 'grapevine' that a shop up Bridge Street in Pendlebury was selling fireworks. Fireworks! They were just something adults talked about, we hadn't seen them throughout the war, although the pyrotechnics on blitz nights took some beating!

Anyway we all rushed off to this shop and joined the queue comprised of just about every other child in the town which stretched, seemingly, for miles. All I had in the world was three old pence. I queued for ages, got my three penny bangers and rushed home to get ready for that night's bonfire celebration in the field opposite our house. We had known the war was due to end anytime and so were ready with one of the biggest bonfires anybody had ever seen.

Came the night, the bonfire was lit and all the lads started getting bits of smouldering wood to use to 'light the blue touch-paper'. Nothing. Everyone was a dud having got damp in that shop cellar throughout the war. The fire was good though — and the blackened roast potatoes!

Fire fascinates all kids, but we used to do some crazy things when I was young and we used to play some crazy games as well.

Every summer when the grass was dry from the long hot days we ALWAYS used to have then one of our gang nip home and 'steal' a match from the box next to the kitchen stove or on top of the mantle-piece — it depended how tall you were and how high the mantle-piece was which target you

Salford motor bus, as used on Swinton routes 1936-1939.

aimed for.

The thief would then rejoin the waiting gang in the middle of the field and the match would be lit on a stone with the whole group crowding round to make sure a sudden gust didn't blow it out (we were so scared of being found out that we only dared steal one match at a time.)

The match lit, it was then applied to the dry grass and what we called 'sweeling' (although I don't think any of us knew how to spell it or where the word originated. The fire would spread outward as it ate into the grass and we would try to create an ever widening ring by lighting other lumps of grass all around us. Needless to say unless it was a very, very still day, the grass only burnt in the direction the breeze was blowing.

Now this was a relatively safe operation until some idiot got ambitious and started to make fires all over the field with burning torches of grass. Very soon everything would get out of hand, we would panic and start beating the fires out with our jackets — despite knowing the dire consequences of going home with a scorched coat later. Most of the time we managed to put the fires out but sometimes we failed and hedges and fences would start to burn. That would mean the calling out of the fire brigade by some disturbed neighbour and a group of very frightened youngsters making themselves very scarce. We never learned, though, because I remember we did the same thing year after year.

Going back to the valley, the cutting led to the 'Black Harry' tunnel on a line that linked Eccles and Patricroft by a devious route to Bolton. The tunnel ran right under the town from Swinton to Pendlebury. During the war it was used as a munitions store and had huge guarded gates across the entrance.

After the war the gates went and the railway tunnel became disused. It was a real dare to walk the length of that dripping tunnel and, believe me, it was dangerous because there were uncovered manholes all over the place. The only safe way was to walk along the centre of the tracks on the 'sleepers' (why were they never the right distance apart for a normal stride?) and risk tripping up. We never had sufficient light to make that journey in real safety — usually all we could manage was one feeble torch which the owner would use to lead the way, the rest of us stumbling along behind like a school 'crocodile'. What a triumph to reach the other end with an intermediary sigh of relief when at long last the light at the other end of the tunnel came in view.

We never went back home the same way, though, preferring the safety of the overground route, and anyway, most times the torch batteries were flat.

On one occasion when we got a little older I recall us going down to the tunnel and letting off fireworks inside to create a bigger bang. Some years later, as a young reporter, I covered the story of that tunnel collapsing and dragging several houses into the yawning hole and killing several residents. Just thinking of the risks we took earlier in that old tunnel which had not been maintained for years, was quite frightening.

There was a 12ft high wall which ran along the boundary of one of our fields and cut off a housing estate on the other side. It would be about 200 ft long and we regularly climbed on to its foot wide top and balanced our way along. It was not that simple because there were overhanging tree branches to be negotiated and irate housewives telling us to get down didn't help. They never seemed to realise that the drop on the other side was the same as the one on their's and got fairly 'ratty' when we didn't immediately obey orders.

Nobody fell off that wall but many fell off the fence rails on the golf course boundary as we balanced along them and many was the bruised body that landed at the bottom of a rather steep slope if they fell on the wrong 'side'.

The field within the wall housed a fair number of cart horses used by a greengrocer to haul his delivery carts around town and often we would lure the unsuspecting animals to the fence with bits of bread and then climb on their backs and ride bare-back around the field — again falling off with alarming regularity. Often an adult would 'snitch' on us to the police and I remember Sgt. Foxall used to creep along the hedge to catch us at it. He was good, too, because he often grabbed us before we saw him and had chance to run away.

I remember Sgt. Foxall well. He was a thin man with ginger hair and always rode around on a bike. I never remember him without bicycle clips around his trouser bottoms. Why he always appeared when we were in trouble and not one of the other 'bobbies' I could never understand. He pulled me home once by the ear for giving him cheek and my father, being a special constable at that time, had to give me a very public walloping for my sins. It's not easy not crying when your friends are all watching agog.

We were always climbing trees. That part was easy. The getting down was harder. There were always constant cries of 'I'm stuck' from the the more adventurous who climbed too high and then

On my bike with a friend in Cumberland St. Lower Broughton.

there would be the rigmarole of those on the ground guiding them down with voices of encouragement. 'Another six inches with your right foot'… 'If you drop now you'll land on that branch two foot below you'… Stop crying or we'll fetch your mam' and so it went.

I do recall one occasion concerning trees when one unfortunate in the gang didn't get stuck but was made to stay up the tree by the rest of the gang prodding him with poles. Despite his pleas we didn't believe him until he finally proved his point by doing something unfortunate in his trousers. We all made ourselves scarce again as his, understandably, angry mother sought us out. Mind you he got into even more trouble from us later for 'telling' on us!

Climbing, wading, crawling, riding, running, sliding… we made our way around in many many ways in those golden childhood days when fear of sinister attacks were virtually unheard of.

46

Chapter Eight

Our Gang's War & Games

People used to sometimes remark that 'so-and-so had had a good war' — well our gang's war wasn't so bad!

I remember the air raids and the fact that if they went on for over an hour you were allowed to go to school an hour later the next day. Fancy wanting an air raid to last over an hour — we did!

After every air raid the next morning would see little lads (girls never seemed to bother) scouring the pavements and gutters for little pieces of metal. Shrapnel, it was, and highly prized if it had some recognisable marking on it showing it definitely came from shell or bomb and wasn't just a jagged piece of metal. We hoarded it like gold and it became one of the main forms of barter in our childlike society — along with old comics that is.

But if shrapnel was prized it had nothing on the fins of incendiary bombs and bullet cases and I remember I once had a incendiary bomb 'stick'. In those days any other child would have given me his whole collection for that. It got thrown out as 'rubbish' by my mother after it had lain forgotten in the garage for years.

And then as the war progressed we started to collect army cap badges and badges of rank and other military insignia. I remember the badges of the Scottish regiments — which always seemed twice the size of the English ones and also always seemed to have stags with a full set of antlers on them — were the most highly prized at first.

Later, when the Yanks came their badges were worth about double that of the Brits (particularly the officers' eagle badges) in the 'swaps' market and even later, when the spoils of victory started seeping through, getting German badges and medals was the only way of securing badge collecting credibility with your mates.

But the war wasn't all fun. Those long hours in the shelters could get dreary and boring (no portable radios and personal cassette players in those days), especially if you were banned from going to the door of the shelter to watch the searchlights and gun flashes. It was quite a piece of subterfuge to be able to sneak out from a shelter containing about ten people. I didn't manage it very often but when I did what a thrill I got.

You could stay in the shadows and listen to the adults having a smoke at the top of the steps and talking about what was going on. 'That's one of theirs', someone would say, 'you can tell by the engine note.' (Do readers remember the different notes of 'ours' and the German planes. Theirs never seemed to be synchronised).

Someone else would say 'Trafford Park's copping it' or 'It's Liverpool's turn tonight' as the bombers passed harmlessly overhead.

I've mentioned before that we lived fairly high up and overlooked Trafford Park — the big industrial complex which contributed so much to the war effort. Seeing the fires start as the bombs dropped and seeing them still burning the next day is something I will never forget.

Our parents hated it when the mobile gun stopped near our house. For one thing it usually meant a crop of shattered windows and for another it brought fears of German retribution if they could target it. It seemed the best way to avoid all this was to 'brew-up' for the gun crew — they couldn't fire the gun AND drink tea could they?

We had a barrage balloon site quite close by manned by Waafs (as they were then called) and watching the balloon being serviced and going up and down provided endless hours of interest (and cat-calling when they got it wrong). They seemed to do most of it for practice, though, and not very often 'in anger'.

The girls lived in two Nissen huts and were always being pestered by the 'big lads'. At least we thought they were being pestered, on reflection they might have been enjoying the attention who knows — we were too young for such things, dammit.

And then the Yanks came. The nearest they came to us was Worsley Green just a few miles away but their camp was like a magnet. Every available opportunity we would be down there noses to the fencing uttering the well-known cries of 'Got any gum, chum' or 'Got any Yankee comics mister'. They were generous to a fault even though they must have been heartily sick of being 'mithered' at by every kid for miles around.

Funny how the urchin's grapevine works because on the day they upped camp ready for the invasion of Europe I guarantee every child from every nearby town, who wasn't languishing in a sick bed or had a totally intransigent mother,

heard about the move and was there clamouring for goodies. I remember seeing the film 'Yanks' some time ago when the same thing was portrayed and believe me it was exactly like that. I hate to think how many convoys it took to bring over the sweets, gum and comics that those guys threw over the backs of their lorries to us. What an anti-climax when they were gone.

As I say the gang had a 'good war'. I cannot remember any father not coming back intact or any house being too badly damaged (apart from the local shops) although everyone seemed to have suffered some effects of incendiary bombs and blast.

As the years went by the hoards of shrapnel and badges slipped away to goodness knows where along with the cigarette cards, the toy soldiers and the wind-up train sets. But I am a great hoarder and I still have a few treasured items including a Royal Artillery cap badge with a gun wheel that moves and a couple of Iron Crosses. Strange to think that I have had them now for nearly 50 years.

I referred to the 'urchin's grapevine' last week and that started me thinking about other things that the 'grapevine' knew instinctively.

It was uncanny how the 'grapevine' let every child know that yesterday was the end of the skipping season and that today spinning tops were in. Or that marbles were out and conkers were in.

How it happened I could never understand but it did. One day you held the record for the number of 'peppers' you could endure while skipping and the next day you were nothing if you couldn't send a spinning top ten feet. We boys disdained the 'beehive' tops which were regarded as being tame

A happy little soul wasn't I?

and for girls only and instead went for the 'flyers' with the thin shank and round top which, if hit perfectly, would fly through the air to the danger of everyone within yards. Naturally our combative attitude meant that something like a league table was drawn up (with points deducted for every broken window) as to who held the title for sending the top the farthest, or highest, or actually managed to hit someone.

Then there were marbles. We would spend endless hours flipping marbles along the gutter (no fudging allowed) trying to hit our opponents and the ground rules for those games were legion. No 'clayeys' were allowed — those were the ones that disintegrated if hit too fiercely and had no part in the collection of any self-respecting marbles player. No steelies (ball bearings) were allowed because they were too heavy and could rarely be knocked out of a chalked circle by a glass marbles. I remember we used to call marbles 'alleys' but I never did know why.

Boys would walk along with canvas bags rattling invitingly and goading others into games of 'skill'. I saw more fights over marbles than anything else as a child. It just seemed to bring out the worst in people.

Conkers came a close second though, particularly if you failed to hold the target conker steady. You would steep the conkers in vinegar, put them in the oven, keep them out of the light for a year to wither and harden — in fact anything to get an advantage over an opponent.

If you were successful in disintegrating an opponent's conker your conker took on that score as well so that if you had a 'tenner' and knocked out a 'fiver' yours then became a 'fifteener' and you were in the market for some big league contests. I wonder if children do that today. I suppose they must for there is a chestnut tree near where I live which gets a severe battering every season as the local children throw sticks, stones and any other handy missiles up into the tree to dislodge the conkers. You never seem to see them playing conkers in the street though — perhaps it's confined to school playgrounds these days.

When I was young we had a collection of old records for our wind-up gramophone — the sort where you had to change the steel needle every few records and drop the old needles into the little canvas bag set into the top of the player. I remember I used to love emptying the bag and collecting the old needles although I can't remember ever finding a use for them. We had wooden needles too which had a little sharpener with them. They didn't seem to stay in vogue for long though.

Anyway along came the more sophisticated recordings and equipment and the old records were regarded as surplus and became available for other things. I remember being shown how to make tulip and daffodil bowls out of old records by putting them into the oven and melting them to just the right consistency so that they became pliable. You could then fashion them into bowls with wavy edges. The hole in the middle became the hole in the bottom — excellent for drainage.

Once I got the knack of this I made hundreds of the things. We had some very thick single sided records which were excellent and much stronger than the rest. I bet those records would be worth a king's ransom now. Ah well! I wonder if modern LPs — soon to suffer the same fate with the advent of Compact Discs — will also make bowls. I know they are made of a different substance now so I'm not prepared to try, but somebody might.

And then we used to make 'piggies' out of bits of wood. Piggies were little sticks sharpened at one end which you laid on a brick or similar object and hit with another bigger stick (something like a small baseball bat). The idea was to flip the 'piggy' into the air and then hit it as far as you could. Furthest away was the winner. We always seemed to be sending missiles through the air in those days, tops, piggies, arrows, stone from catapults — it's a wonder more people didn't get hurt!

Piggy had a season too and would end as soon as it had started once the 'grapevine' said so.

We haunted the local electrical shop in Station Road in Swinton which stocked endless reels of thin wire in a variety of colours because we discovered a way of plaiting the strands to make multi-coloured 'bracelets' which were highly prized by the girls and put you in their good books if you made them a good one. Gosh even in those young days the girls had us hooked.

And then there were the fluffy balls we could make by winding old lengths of wool round the cardboard milk bottle tops of those days and then snipping the ends. They didn't have much practical use but they looked nice.

Talking of milk bottle tops. People always seem to have trouble opening those cardboard packs of milk which seem to be sold everywhere now. I seem to remember getting many a 'shower' when the little hole in the middle of the cardboard tops didn't yield to 'gentle' pressure and suddenly spurted everywhere.

Apart from constantly fashioning the latest fighter and bomber aeroplanes out of assorted odds and ends of wood I remember we used to make 'tanks' out of old cotton reels. We would nick the edges of the reel to make 'tracks', slip an elastic band through the hole in the middle and at one end fit a half matchstick and a stub of candle and at the other a full matchstick. Once you wound the elastic taut and let it go the full match would act as a 'drive' and propel the tank along. Great fun they were. Having battle with them was rather like those tricks you see with plates on the ends of sticks. You always seemed to be winding and winding to keep the things in 'action'.

What else did we do? Well we played 'How many strides to the lion's den?' 'Farmer, farmer, many we cross your field?' both of which involved forfeits and often necessitated the girls showing items of underwear to prove they were wearing the required colour — but enough of that! Then we played 'Rally-heave-ho' which usually meant spending most of the playtime running around in groups arms linked shouting, 'Who will be on our side?' By the time the question had been answered and the teams decided it was usually 'bell time' and we had to go back to classes. However the sides had been picked and the game could continue straightaway in the afternoon break.

Now the game meant that the side losing the toss had to stand in a 'crocodile' facing a wall — strongest at the front — to make a back for the opponents to leap on. They ran and jumped on the waiting backs, the best jumpers going first, to get as far up the backs as possible. The winning side was the one which held most bodies without collapsing. Great fun I must say!

As I walk around in the evenings the thing that strikes me most is the flickering lights coming from the houses I pass, which is always a sure sign that the occupants are watching television.

Now that is no bad thing. I am not one of those people who think that television is a one eyed monster in the corner which is dominating our lives. What does sadden me about such sights is that the viewing starts so early, even in the long evenings of summer.

Now I know we live in dangerous times, but there can't be a child molester or abductor on every corner and yet you so rarely see children playing out in the street. The one eyed monster had got them!

In my youth the streets were never empty of children playing. There was a pattern to it. Home from school, a quick drink and a 'butty' and then out to indulge in whatever game or pastime was the current favourite.

Girls would purloin their mother's washing lines or, more usually, assemble a decent length of skipping rope from the remains of several cast off lines. These would be tied together by fiercesome knots which caused more than a little pain if they struck your legs when you failed to jump high enough. Yes, boys did join in their skipping but only the macho 'peppers' or using the rope as a 'high jump' (lots of scarred knees resulted from that pursuit), the soft stuff, the 'dolly' skipping, we left to the girls.

At various corners of the streets the girls would be playing with dolls and creating imaginary 'shops' where imaginary goods were sold — they had to be imaginary, there were no goods to spare for childish pastimes during the 30s and 40s. Now it is a common sight to see groups of children at garden gates indulging in their own version of a car boot sale and selling all sorts of unwanted toys and books.

Lads would zoom as close as they could to these 'shops' on their bikes just for the fun of making the girls scream. Often the too daring lads would come a cropper and limp home trying all the time not to cry and lose face constantly repeating (loudly, but not very convincingly) "It didn't hurt me, it didn't hurt me". Once round the corner and out of sight, though, it was often a different story. That reminds me of the 'badges of courage' lads seemed to always bear. I am referring to the plasters and bandages which seemed to cover every knee and elbow. I also remember the torture of getting those plasters off tender skin later. You would pull at a corner a little at a time, then try another corner until gradually there was only a little left sticking to your body. Then you could have a final tug. I remember my father seeing me doing that once and coming up to "have a look" only to pull the plaster off in one go. I yelped and cried and after that always made sure I tugged those plasters off out of sight.

Little or no traffic to disrupt those games (I wonder if that and not television is why children no longer play in the streets — even the back streets now seem to have traffic jams and drivers use them as 'rat runs' to avoid the congestion on main roads). The games went on and on, particularly in summer, with one reluctant player after another being called in for bedtime or homework. It usually needed several callings and dire threats about the consequences before the chosen child left the pack and went towards a mother standing on the corner arms akimbo with

Reminiscent of the Salford back alleys I knew as a child — only we didn't the television aerials then!

a look that said they would brook no intransigence.

And the games. 'Farmer, farmer, may we cross your field?', 'How many strides to the lion's den?' 'What time is it Mr Wolf?' 'Rally Heaveo' which seemed to have a different name and slightly different rules district by district, hopscotch, French cricket, whipping tops, marbles, skipping, kick-ball hide, even digging tar out of the gaps in the cobbles with sticks when the weather was really hot and then seeing who could create the biggest tar ball. That was fun, but the aftermath wasn't because it usually meant using precious butter to rid soiled hands of the sticky substance.

For the boys there was football, of course, with the inevitable crop of broken windows and forays into gardens to retrieve the ball all the time expecting (and usually receiving) retribution from irate householders. There were roller skating and bogey races on home made trucks constructed from planks and old pram wheels and finally swings on the iron lamp on the street corner.

For years I thought that iron bar sticking out from the top of the lamp had been put there by some thoughtful designer just so lads could throw a rope over it and swing to their hearts content. It was, of course, there so that repair men could prop a ladder against it and climb up the ladder to carry out repairs. What a mundane use for such a marvellous appendage.

Carefree days and the only problems being created by the 'miseries', and there were always a few, who didn't like to see children enjoying themselves and certainly didn't like having their windows broken!

There were hundreds of other games and pastimes which helped fill our days. Many of them seem to have disappeared now. It seems to be all skateboards today — although I suppose they are just an extension of our 'bogies' and 'books on skates'. The only difference is that we made them ourselves.

Yes television and modern crime waves have got a lot to answer for — the principle ones being robbing the children of today of the childhood experiences I enjoyed which were so memorable. I think all children should grow up like that. The 'box' is educational and entertaining. It's good — but not that good.

Nostalgia is a funny thing though I like to think we had more fun in my young days. I mean how many people over 45 can't remember the thrill of 'Postman's Knock' when you, at last, picked the right number and got the girl of your choice into the hall for one of those hard lipped kisses which were all we seemed to know about in those innocent days. They may be more sophisicated at their birthday parties now — with presents for those going home for goodness sake! — but things like that took some beating.

Chapter Nine

Food, Treats, & Shopping

Food and treats. Thinking about them brings back a flood of memories.

Nuttalls Mintoes! Still going strong today and still unchanged in appearance and taste. Just going for a 2oz bag of Mintoes in the middle thirties in Harpurhey, Manchester, was an adventure because I had to cross a main road! I'm not altogether sure I was supposed to do that but the shop on my side of the road didn't stock Mintoes and Mintoes it had to be, so what was a lad to do? I would cast caution to the winds and dart across to the corner shop. On reflection, as those were the days mostly of horse and cart transport, I don't suppose I was in much danger, but it certainly felt like it to that small boy.

And then there were the Saturday afternoon matinees which always necessitated buying sustenance to see us through the two hour show. This was at a later age when walking along the main road was allowed — as long as you were in a group — although in reality groups were far more dangerous as someone was always being shoved into the road as we larked about.

So the gang would invade the corner shop on the way to the cinema (or pictures as we called them) and drive the shop-keeper wild while we agonised over penny lucky bags, sherbet dips, dolly mixtures, liquorice pinwheels and pipes and all the other goodies that were on offer. No wonder we all had bad teeth, those sweets must have beeen a dentist's nightmare.

Then to the cinema and the sharing would begin. Deciding the value of half a dozen dolly mixtures against a suck on the sherbet dip was agonising. And letting someone have a dip into your penny lucky bag in exchange for a bit on a liquorice pinwheel — well!

But during the war treats were few and far between, If I remember rightly we were allowed a quarter of sweets a month! We usually saved the treat for once a month and then spent ages gazing at the goods on offer in the sweetshop window balancing the longevity of aniseed balls against barley sugars. One of the stopgaps in those days were liquorice roots. You could chew them with jaw aching monotony for hours until all you were left with was a stringy yellow substance that looked most unappetising and probably was. To toffee starved kids, though, they were a lifeline.

I must confess that my mother was not the best cook in the world — but we survived. I suppose things were difficult for any woman during the war but sadly the economic habits of those days were carried over into peacetime with disastrous culinary results.

Two things I do remember with pleasure. One was the 'fry-up' of the vegetables left over from Sunday dinner which, with some corned beef, would make a tasty Monday evening meal. The other was mother's meat and potato pie (with crust) which went down a treat with pickled red cabbage. Her secret was to add corned beef to the stewing meat. I still look forward to that dish today (the recipe was passed on to my wife).

First thing we did when we came home from school was to ask for a 'butty'. Children call them all sorts of different things throughout the country — I believe in the North East they call them 'pieces'. Anyway our choice was jam (not bad) marmalade (passable) beef dripping (rarely) or 'sugar butties (glorious) which were made from a slice of bread (hopefully the crust) with butter and then sprinkled with sugar. Again a dentist's nightmare but unsurpassable to a child.

School dinners were regarded with horror but, I suppose, provided us with a staple diet during, and for a long time after, the war. We put up with them but only went back for 'seconds' when it was syrup sponge with custard or, maybe, rice pudding with a spoonful of jam in the middle.

I was, for a time, school milk monitor in my last year at the junior school and that meant delivering the half-pint milk bottles to the various classes for mid-morning break along with the straws which never seemed to last more than two sucks before they collapsed.

The real treat in being milk monitor (and there were always two of us) was that there always seemed to be at least half a dozen extra bottles left over. If you weren't quick the teachers would grab them for their tea making but if you were a bit nimble (and we were) you could hide them to savour later in the day or even barter them for some other treats. I know I always seemed to be awash with milk in those days.

Finally there were the 'treats' my grandmother used to bring home. She was a waitress in Lewis's store in the middle of Manchester in the grand days when they had an orchestra and all the visiting music hall stars used to eat there. (I've still got an autograph from G.H. Elliot, the 'Chocolate Coloured Coon'). This was just after the war and every night she would empty her shopping bag revealing a crushed Kunzle cake or two (remember them?) which obviously were too far gone to be offered to a customer — there seemed to be a heck of a lot of crushed cakes in those days — there would be loose biscuits which a customer had left on his plate and which could not be returned for resale, odd fruit items and single cigarettes which customers would leave instead of a financial tip in those days of shortages.

I was an early smoker and once I found where those odd cigarettes were hidden (at the bottom of grandmother's wardrobe) I was never short of the odd underage 'drag'. It's amazing how long a cigarette can last when you only keep taking two puffs and then 'dimp' it out to keep for another occasion. I got too ambitious in my 'liberating' of those cigarettes and finally grandmother (reluctantly) had to tell my father... the punishment he meted out was well deserved.

I wonder if we are destroying our immune systems by being too cautious about the preparation, packaging and display of food? Salmonmella and listeria scares prompted the thought and set me thinking about the way food was prepared and sold in the 30s and 40s.

There used to be a shop on Chorley Road in Swinton which sold just about everything edible apart from fish — and it was all in one deliciously mouth-watering array with raw meat alongside cooked meats with the odd open tin of loose biscuits nudging a pile of sausages. I suppose someone will tell me it was a potentially lethal food-poisoning mixture but I never heard of anyone being made ill from any of their purchases.

And the stuff they sold! Brawn (never ask what it's made of just enjoy the taste), pigs trotters, cow heels, tripe, and potted meats of all kinds not in those fiddly little pots you get now but served from white glazed bowls the contents always having a layer of fat to seal the flavour in.

There would be breads of every description and barm cakes. It was nothing for the shop assistant to serve up some tripe or cowheels, give the hands a quick wipe on an apron and then prepare a filled barmcake for a hungry child. There was a bus-stop right outside the shop and you always had to keep an eye out for the driver getting in his cab. If that happened you fled the shop and left shop assistant 'holding the baby'. If they recognised you the next time you went in, though, you 'copped it'. For a while after events like that it was policy to send in a friend to make the purchase even though it usually meant you having to let him have a bite — usually a huge one — from your purchase.

There would be sausages of all shapes and sizes — and fillings — along with black puddings and, one of my favourites — polony. I used to love peeling the red outer skin from polony to get at the soft meat inside. Crumpets and potato cakes (I note the posh word for them now is 'farles') and muffins vied for space with those huge square tins of Huntley and Palmer loose biscuits. We used to get an 'assortment' by buying a few from each tin long before the manufacturers cottoned on to the possibilities.

Go in a grocery shop now and you might just find four sauce varieties on offer. We had dozens. H.P. Daddies, O.K. (Master O.K. the Saucy Boy) Yorkshire Relish, Lea and Perrins, Tiger the names were legion and many of them manufactured locally. There were pickles of every description — again produced locally at the Norco factory — and cooked meats. You could get slices of beef, pork (always accompanied by a piece of crackling), tongue, delicious hams, corned beef, we didn't go in much for turkey and chicken pieces in those days but at Christmas you could hardly see the shop frontage for the number of birds suspended on hooks, again not very hygienic but impressive, and none of it was 'hermetically sealed'. It was wrapped in whatever came to hand and off you went. I know one or two places where you can still get many of those foods but they are isolated from each other in refrigerated cabinets and are sold alongside Indian bhajis, samosas and mortadella!

I remember bread was never wrapped — and sliced bread hadn't appeared at that time. If you were sent for a loaf it was usually still warm when you got it and totally irrestible on the way home. Many's the loaf I have presented to my mother with the bottom corners nibbled away. Honest Mum it was like that.

And if you went for the bread you had the treat of having the crust with a bewildering choice of toppings, beef dripping, sauce, jam, marmalade, cheese or, my favourite — sugar! If the sliced crust was thick enough it earned the title 'docker's wedge' from my father.

You knew what day it was by the food on the table. Fry-up on Monday's from the Sunday meal left-overs, usually fish on Friday even if you were not in a Catholic household and potato pie with a crust and lashing of pickled red cabbage on Saturday lunch times to put you in fine fettle for the football terraces in the afternoon. When things were tight you usually got 'pobs' a mixture of bread and milk but, thankfully, that didn't happen too often, I used to hate the stuff!

Just further along the road was a fishmongers and he, too, was no respecter of hygiene rules. The front of the shop opened totally to the street with all the traffic between Manchester and the North streaming constantly passed. People would pick the fish up and smell it, tentatively weigh it in their hands and then either put it back — more often than not — or march into the shop to have it weighed and wrapped. I suppose such goings on would send shivers of horror down some people now but it was part of the daily routine.

The local town centre butchers used to do their own slaughtering in tiny back street buildings and the meat was stored on huge blocks of ice — no refrigerators then — and then transported on the backs of assistants through the streets to the shops.

And talking of refrigerators (or lack of them and, by the way, do readers remember meat safes?) reminds me of one familiar scene at home. Milk constantly went sour — it doesn't go sour now it just goes bad — and the only use for it was to make it into cottage cheese by putting it in muslin bags and hanging it from the beams in the washhouse. We always seemed to have dozens of those dripping bags around and if you were unwary you got a soggy faceful. I detested that stuff as well and nothing would persuade me to try it however hungry I was — I think I was about 45 before I even attempted to eat the modern cottage cheeses and I quite like them now!

I was saddened to read a newspaper report recently that coffee has now replaced tea as the great British beverage. I never thought I would see the day because it seemed that when I was growing up everybody was constantly brewing up or 'mashing' tea as they say in some parts of the North.

I can remember mother coming in loaded with two heavy baskets of shopping and dropping everything to put the kettle on. At my grandmother's house which had an old fashioned hob the kettle was permanently hot and took but a few seconds to come to the boil.

There was a ritual about brewing up. The tea pot had to be warmed first and there were constant arguments about whether the milk went in first or afterwards and some people even warmed the tea cups (or usually thick mugs) before pouring in the tea. This was in the pre-health conscious days and it was common for someone to ask for three sugars. Four might cause slightly raised eyebrows but it was certainly not uncommon.

I can remember my father sitting reading (or rather devouring) his newspaper and making the laconic comment: "It's a dry ship is this". This was a signal for my mother to immediately stop whatever she was doing and brew up — it was also pre women's lib days as well!

Workmen could be seen with a brew can fastened to their belt containing tea which was either taken cold later or warmed up on some brazier at the work site. Usually the brew was accompanied by a package of cold bacon 'butties'

— enough to make a dietician wince.

Brewing up still seems to be the pre-occupation of a large part of the population — witness the inactivity at most road works sites — but now it seems they are provided with proper brewing facilities including calor gas stoves.

And then there was the supper drink. Milk didn't keep — no fridges then — and whereas now it goes plain bad then it went sour almost with the speed of light. Mother would insist the milk was 'used up' before morning and so we had milk based drinks forced upon us. Ovaltine was standard, although I was put off the stuff by having to listen to the Ovaltinies twittering away on the radio, Horlicks was for special occasions — particularly if you had been 'off colour' but most times it was cocoa or drinking chocolate. Coffee — never.

In fact the only 'coffee' I can recall at all featured a Highland soldier on the label being served with a steaming cup of the brew by a servant. It was called Camp coffee and actually boasted that it contained chicory!

I blame the demise of the great British institution on tea bags. They have taken the ritual out of brewing up and put it in the same arena as fast foods. No tea pots (although I know someone who still puts the tea bags in a teapot first because he likes to do things the traditonal way) and in many cases sweeteners have replaced sugar — health fads again. I understand they are bringing out round tea bags and tea bags with tags on them although what good gimmicks like that will do I don't know. It is forecast that tea drinking will go down by another 16 per cent within the next five years — sad, very sad.

Chapter Ten

Christmas Past

My childhood Christmases were working class Christmases and many of them were in war-time and spent in Salford and Swinton.

Christmas in those days didn't start as early as it seems to do today — immediately after the August Bank Holiday (I noticed that the festive lights in London were switched on in the first week in November and Manchester was not far behind) — in fact you didn't really begin to think about it until school broke up for the holidays — apart, that is, from the odd foray into the bottom of various wardrobes to just feel the odd parcel you found but not to actually spoil things by looking what was in them.

Christmas trees were rare indeed and I recall my family having a pitiful looking silver tree about 18 inches high which had to do as a celebration point for many a year. We loaded it with home made decorations but it still looked a pathetic apology for a Christmas tree.

You couldn't put much around the base of it as we do today. Our practice was to hang a stocking — a football one because it was the biggest — on the foot of the bed and see what next morning brought. It was only after the war, when things became more plentiful, that we gravitated to pillow cases to hold the extra goodies.

Usually there wasn't a lot in those stockings. Before the war it would be the inevitable orange and apple and, hopefully, a box of lead soldiers if you were a boy and a doll if you were a girl. No feminist clap trap in those days.

Do you remember those lead soldiers by the way. Usually within half an hour they had lost their heads and had to be repaired with matchsticks. They made quite realistic 'casualties' in our war games though.

In Salford it was our custom to travel into Manchester on Christmas Eve to try to out-smart the market traders on Smithfield Market. The game was to do a quick tour of the stalls at about 9p.m. as the traders were shutting up shop and try to get them to bring their prices down. It was a game all round really because they knew how low they would go and we knew how low to push them. Satisfying, though, to think you had a bargain.

But before the trip round the market you would start with a toffee apple and then have a wide-eyed tour watching the pot stall men juggling with the plates and cups (there used to be one on Salford Market who revelled in the name of 'Barmy Mick'), listening to the carpet salesmen banging (often in clouds of dust) their rolls of carpets and seemingly offering the wares at ridiculously low prices. There was the Tib Street pet market from where many a pup became a Christmas present only to end up in a sack in the canal at a later date. I remember that canal in Salford. It ran to Bolton and Bury and always seemed to be full of dead animals and old mattresses. There were fish in it though. I know because I caught a few there in later years although how they survived all that pollution I'll never know.

But back to Christmas. The vegetables would be bought, the bird, rarely a turkey more often a chicken from the rather forlorn batch father kept in the back yard, would already have been seen off (I remember some gory tales in later years of chickens still running around our yard with their heads chopped off although as a child I was never allowed to witness such a sight) and the family would make its way back home to prepare for the next day. Not before one final call though and that was to the chestnut man and hot potato man at the top of the street leading to the bus station. What child could resist that smell and what parents could resist the imprecations of the children. So it was a short journey home peeling hot chestnuts and juggling with an extremely hot baked potato in a twist of paper with lots of rough salt in the bottom.

There were always other chestnuts to roast around the open fire. I recall chasing quite a few of them as they exploded and flew across the room. Those fires were 'banked up' to provide a plentiful supply of hot water so the family could all have baths and be clean and presentable for the relatives on Christmas Day. If you had been a 'credit to your mum', as they used to say, relatives were always good for a 'tanner' as they left to go home and that meant more after Christmas treats.

Nowadays many of the small terrace houses have had their 'front rooms' and 'back kitchens' knocked into one to make for a bigger living area. In my childhood the 'front room', or parlour, was only used when relatives called, if one of the older children was doing a bit of courting, or at Christmas. Then the fire would be lit and the room aired in readiness for the family gatherings of uncles, aunts, nieces and nephews who we never set eyes on from one Christmas to the next.

But it was good to have those family gatherings and to exchange gossip. I remember after the Christmas lunch when the conversation started getting serious I would make myself scarce by quietly sliding under the table and curling up among all those legs listening to gossip I was probably not supposed to hear. It's amazing how many of my recollections of past times come from those surreptitious listenings.

Even in wartime we would have a 'good spread' on this one occasion and then would come the games. We were keen on games in my family and every year the same lot would be trotted out and every year the same fun would be had — and family stories told (we had heard them all many times before but they lost nothing in the telling).

We were not a tee-total family but there was never a lot of drink taken — apart from copious amounts of tea (no coffee in those days). Dad always bought in about half a dozen bottles of ale for those who felt the need, there would be a half bottle of whisky (often brought out the next year as well having been unopened), the inevitable sherry and port for the 'aunts' and rum and peppermint — a welcome drink for visitors being sent home on a cold evening. For us kids the treats were hot Vimto or a good glass of Dandelion and Burdock from one of those big stone 'bottles' with a handle.

I suppose these days that sort of Christmas

sounds a bit dull, but I promise you it wasn't. Family ties were important and even though the saying 'you can pick your friends but you can't pick your relatives' often had an edge of truth about it those links did a lot to hold people together in difficult, often hungry, years.

We didn't have stereos, personal tape players, televisions, CDs, long playing records, videos, computer games and the wealth of other types of entertainment available today. We had a wind up gramophone, later converted to electricity, and one radio for the whole household that we bought before the war and had to keep throughout the 'hostilities' as they were called because you couldn't get replacements or parts.

That radio used to seemingly take hours for the valves (yes valves) to warm up. You'd switch on and peer through the canvas type screen at the front as the valves started to glow, a lot of wheeping and whooping and crackling started and slowly, ever so slowly, the voices would come out of the speaker getting stronger and stronger as the set warmed up. Wireless they called it though why I don't know because it was full of wires. We were fortunate in having a next-door neighbour who was a wireless fanatic and he kept our old set going for us.

The radio was a ritual for the whole family at that time. Everyone had to listen because you made a noise on pain of being sent to your cold bedroom if father missed one of Tommy Handley's jokes. I seem to remember they used to always have a half hour comedy programme on before the main news — probably to cheer us up. You would get Happidrome with 'Ramsbottom and Enoch and me' (me being Harry Korris),

Garrison Theatre with Jack Warner — remember 'Mind my bike' — the air waves were full of catch-phrases and frankly how some of the entertainers got away with it I really don't know.

It was these comedy shows that really kept the family at home night after night. I am sure if we measured them that we would all have one ear slightly larger than the other from straining to hear the jokes and patter through the crackles and fadings.

Nat Mills and Bobby, Frank Randle, Norman 'Over the Garden Wall' Evans, Tommy Handley, of course along with Funf, Colonel Chinstrap, 'Can I do yer now sir?', 'I don't mind if I do', 'I go, I come back' and so on and so on. Hundreds of catch phrases that people of my age can still conjure up after all this time.

With his Irish connections father was a devotee of Cavan O'Connor (I'm Only a Strolling Vagabond), Arthur Tracey the 'Street Singer', 'Marta' was the one he always gave us, and Josef Locke who belted out 'Goodbye' with alarming regularity. Gracie Fields was popular coming, as she did, from our neck of the woods and during the war Vera Lynn could do no wrong in our household.

Then we were 'entertained' by Lord Haw Haw' (the traitor William Joyce) and it was always a talking point when he mentioned our area. I know the 'Black Harry tunnel' and its munitions store was mentioned and I recall my parents and friends expressing fears about our proximity to that tunnel full of explosives should Lord Haw Haw's predictions of a raid on it come to pass. Thankfully it never did.

Later we had the wartime shows featuring people like Arthur Askey and Richard 'Stinker' Murdoch, Kenneth Horne in Much Binding in the Marsh ('Tiddley om pom, pom'), Stand Easy (wasn't that with Charlie Chester?), Bandwagon, Monday Night at Eight — 'Carry on London' — oh there were hundreds and hundreds of people offering radio entertainment.

On the musical side there was Charlie Kunz, Henry Hall's Guest Night, Bill — Wakey, Wakey — Cotton, Carroll Gibbons, Hutch, Jack Payne, Ivy Benson and her 'all girl' band and, of course, Glenn Miller. As they say, 'They don't make them like that anymore.'

And that wind-up gramophone. During the war we had to make do with records we had bought in the 30s. Many of them were thick single sided affairs and they were all scratched and hissy. It was entertainment to our unsophisticated selves, though, and bought a lot of fun. I can still recall mother and father in a fit of silliness getting up from their armchairs one time and giving the family a demonstration of the Charleston with the necessary hands crossing on knees and thumb licking. Oh my.

Later when records became available I discovered Hoagy Carmichael and bought and played everything he recorded. I can still recall the words to them all. Still later when girls became an interest the lads would walk home from the pictures, arm round the girl, crooning (as everyone did) their imitations of Nat King Cole and Frank Sinatra. It's a good job we didn't have personal recorders then because had we recorded ourselves as we walked along I don't think any of us would come out of hiding ever again!

We always had the 'relatives' for Sunday tea.

I can't remember us going to them very often apart from the odd foray at Christmas and New Year, no, they always 'came to' us much to my father's disgust and barely disguised disapproval.

I wasn't too happy either because it meant I had to sit around all afternoon being polite when really all I wanted to do was join my friends playing football in the field. Every so often there would be a timid knock on the back door — always the back door for little urchins — and a request 'Is your lad playing out? When I heard the answer 'No' from my mother my heart sank even lower. I had a fellow feeling about it all with my father only in his case it was keeping him out of his beloved shed!

I remember those teas well and only in later life learnt about the 'politics' involved. It seems there was always a preponderance of mother's relatives with father's barely getting a look in and that caused lots of family discontent. The fact that mother had a bigger number of relatives than father seems not to have been an element in the arguments.

Anyway those teas. Never fewer than eight and more often than not twelve sat down at the table on chairs and 'forms' borrowed for the occasion from a local school, carried by me, naturally, after school on the previous Friday.

The 'fare', particularly in the war years, was fairly spartan but there was always plenty of 'fillage' in the shape of bread and 'marge' to make up for the lack of tasty bits.

Often the main item would be boiled ham, or tongue or, in 'flush' times', tinned salmon. No 'starter' — the ubiquitous prawn cocktail or 'soup

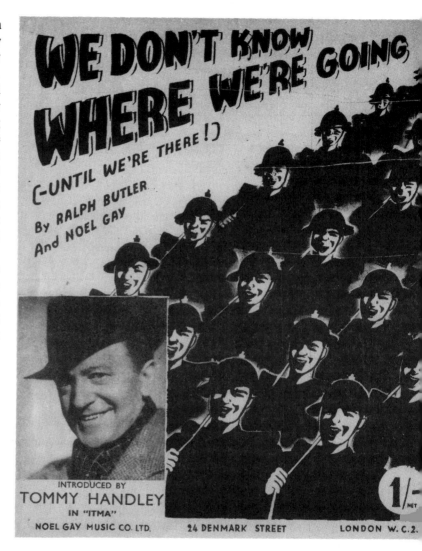

of the day' were a long way off in the future, no, it was just the main meal and a 'sweet.

There would be bowls of lettuce, hard boiled eggs, tomatoes, cucumbers and lots and lots of different pickles. People passed these bowls around and invariably someone got landed with a bowl and no place to put it down! As I say the bread plate did something of a whirling dervish impersonation as it moved around the table. 'Take two slices' was the call, and when the plate was empty (it didn't take long) it was then taken into the kitchen to be refilled — several times.

Strict, though unwritten, rules applied. The men had the lion's share of the main delicacy and there was always something left in the bowls for decency's sake and in case anyone, if they dared, certainly I daren't, asked for seconds.

Pudding was rare. Usually the sweets were pineapple chunks, again if times were good, but most often pear halves accompanied by what mother insisted on calling, much to my irritation, 'Libby's' - evaporated milk. In some cases the Carnation variety was used, same stuff, different name. Cream was unheard of, no fridges to keep it fresh — and strawberries as a delicacy came around once a year and usually only for a fortnight. It wasn't like today when aeroplanes can bring exotic delights from all over the world to our shops and supermarkets and seasons have lost their meaning.

I can recall being sent many times to pick blackberries from the neighbouring field to be used as a 'sweet' when there was nothing else around. And you didn't go to the freezer for the ice-cream either — mainly because there were no freezers — you made starting your sweets coincide with the arrival of the ice cream cart — ours was Noonans and the cart came as regular as clockwork every Sunday afternoon. Out you went with a fruit bowl to have it loaded with scoops of ice cream to be shared out on top of the fruit.

The privilege of having the residue in the bowl always fell to me as did the chance to 'lick the bowl clean' after mother had been mixing cake ingredients.

Uncountable cups of tea throughout the meal, never wine, uncountable cups of tea afterwards and then off they went home with me always standing in a rather importuning way at the front door as they left, not exacxtly holding out my hand but let any relative try to get through that door and past my father's stern gaze without pressing a 'three-penny joey' in my hand!

By the time they had gone the front room fire (it was always the front room on Sundays) was usually just about glowing enough to make toast for supper. It's all done in electric toasters now but we used to stick the bread on the ends of long, and extendable, toasting forks and get each slice exactly as the recipient wanted it — burnt offerings as well. Mind you if the fire was still too hot you, as they say, 'sweated cobs' during the task — and woe betide you if you got careless and let a slice slip off and into the coals!

Chapter Eleven

Clogs & Shawls

It seems strange to think that in the late 30s and even at the beginning of the war in Swinton women were still walking about in shawls and clogs, miners were still to be seen in their pit dirt (few of the mines had pit head baths then) and mill hooters still sounded to call people to work. (Sounds like something out of old Gracie Fields film but it was part of everyday life in the mill and pit towns of Lancashire).

We didn't still have 'knockers-up' as they had had a decade before but I can still remember seeing mill 'girls' finishing their shift at the Acme Mill (gone now) in Pendlebury clattering, yes, clattering on their clogs, through the town, on their way home. I can also remember miners at the end of their shifts squatting down outside the pubs waiting for opening time. They had black faces and grimy clothing but they also had a word for anyone passing — usually coarse.

I wonder if you remember miners in their 'Sunday best'. That usually consisted of a flat cap and a white scarf. The clothes were free of coal dust but that was their only concession to the social graces.

I remember the housewives. You would see them going to the 'beer house' — off-licences or wine stores we call them now — to get a jug of ale to go with their husband's dinner — it was always dinner at mid-day in Swinton. We didn't know the meaning of the word lunch. We had tea at the time the 'gentry' had dinner and supper was usually a

slice of toast and cup of Bovril or Ovaltine before bed.

I read a book by Robert Roberts called 'A Ragged Schooling' and in it he described the women of his time who walked in the streets without a shawl as 'being in their figure' What an apt description of the women of Lancashire in the late 30s.

Everything was done by the rules. Donkey stoning the front steps, wearing the correct garments, preparing the right meals for your husband and children — everything had to be done by the norms of the community and the good Lord help you if you didn't conform. You would be labelled as 'no better than she ought to be' — and try living with that in those times!

I can remember those off-licences. I would go in occasionally doing an 'errand' for my mother or a neighbour (a 'penny for going' was the normal rate) and I can still recall the smell of the places. Stale beer and a confection of bread and meat smells would meet you as you opened the door.

We had another peculiar trade in Swinton and Pendlebury in my younger days and that was Norco pickles. The firm had a factory on Bolton Road in Pendlebury and, as you can imagine, the smells from their processing were pretty strong. If you got on a bus at Swinton Town Hall after it had been on the Norco run you could always tell from the lingering 'perfume' that pervaded the vehicle. It took several trips to and from Manchester before the 'pong' disappeared.

Like any Lancashire town we had our fair share of fish and chip shops and shops where you could get brawn, pressed meat, barm cakes, pig's feet, tripe (remember vinegar and pepper in every hole in the honeycomb variety?) cow-heels and, oh, a vast array of other tasty, but very cheap pieces of animal. It didn't pay to inquire too deeply about which parts of the animals they came from — what you didn't know didn't hurt you and, anyway, they tasted delicious. I confess I was never one for cow heels and pig's trotters but tripe — ah! Again I never fancied it cooked with onions as many did. I liked it raw with, as I say, vinegar in every hole.

I still have a friend who now lives in London

We all knew corner shops like this and the ever attentive owners who ran them.

who, every time he comes North, makes it a 'must' to visit Bury Market and buy a supply of black puddings to take back South with him. Competition on the black pudding front may take titles to other far-off parts but for the true Lancastrian, Bury is THE only place to buy black puddings.

We used to have a lot of UCP (United Cattle Products) shops in every town in Lancashire where you could get cheap and tasty meals. Sadly they have gone now but the memory of their savoury offerings lingers on.

Going back to the fish and chip shops we had one in Park Street in Swinton where the owners still cooked on a coal range in the 1940s when everyone else had converted to gas. It survived, I think, because of the fact that it was quite close to one of the local cinemas and was, thus, on the way home for many folk. The chips were not up to much and they were slow at serving the queues because of their antiquated methods, but they were handy. No, the best chips around were from Kidds at Irlams-o-th-Height but, these were pre a car for nearly every household days remember — you were forced to eat them from newspaper wrapped packages as you walked home — they would never have survived the journey home and still have been warm no matter how fast you ran or how well wrapped they were.

That was another feature of our younger days — going to the cinema and walking home eating chips from a newspaper. We still did it when we were 'courting' — how we could do that and then indulge in a few sloppy kisses and imagine it was romantic I can 't think — still it was the same for everyone

There is a famous scene in Hobson's Choice, the film of the Harold Brighouse's play starring Charles Laughton, which is set in the 1890s, when a young couple, played by John Mills and Brenda de Banzie, stand outside the church before their wedding with their guests. In full view behind them are the steaming cooling towers of an electricity power station — Bradford, Manchester I think.

This production clanger set me thinking about the problems modern film producers must have in filming period pieces given the rapid disappearance of old and revered buildings and their equally rapid replacement by what Prince Charles refers to as 'carbuncles' which, undoubtedly, will not stand the test of time. As a matter of fact the Hobson's Choice producer would not now be led into that silly mistake — the cooling towers have been demolished.

One of our local amateur dramatic societies are to stage 'Love on the Dole' that classic by Walter Greenwood set in the slums of Salford in the depression years. On stage they will get away with it because it is still relatively easy to recreate interiors of houses of the period by the usual ploy of making begging public announcements for the loan of old family 'hand-me-downs' which many sentimentalists such as myself still keep. But what of the exteriors?

'Hanky Park', Hankinson Street and the vast area of surrounding slum streets in Salford which was the outdoor setting for the original film in 1941 has long since been replaced by modern monstrosities which, as in many other cities, confine the elderly to lives of isolation in vandal ridden high rises. You really have to scour the

North for houses of the 'Hanky Park' type now and even if you find the odd street they have mostly been 'tarted up' as they say in Lancashire with horrors such as 'stone' cladding (Vera and Jack Duckworth in Coronation Street are not alone in perpetrating such outrages) or the windows will have been modernised and double glazed. But that's not all. How will the producer persuade occupants to get rid of their television aerials and the ever-sprouting satellite dishes during 'shooting' — that will cost a pretty penny in compensation.

No the film producers of tomorrow, should they wish to create old Salford streets (or those of any other Northern town for that matter) for yet another classic remake are going to have to rebuild a whole district for their filming. I can just see 'Hanky Park', Ellor Street and Salford Hippodrome being recreated on some film lot — all facade and supports at the back like on the American movie lots. But ah, where are they going to get the smoke and grime from. I bet recreating that atmosphere would task even the most proficient props man.

There's another lovely line in Hobson's Choice, filmed in 1953 by the way, when Henry

Typical of the 'back entries' in the town I knew so well.

Hobson, (Charles Laughton) is telling his daughter and her new husband Willy Mossop (John Mills) of his troubles. 'Ee', says Willy, ''appen it'll be reported in 't Salford City Reporter.' Henry stirs himself and replies: 'When ruin and disaster overwhelm a man of my importance it's reported in't Manchester Guardian not in't Salford Reporter.' Well Manchester long ago lost it's 'Manchester' Guardian and when I last saw it the Salford City Reporter was a disappointing tabloid which had none of the stature and dignity of the City Reporter of my youth. Poor old Henry Hobson.

I would recommend one foray for prospective film producers trying to recreate the old Salford atmosphere and that is a trip to Lark Hill Place where the wise Corporation of old recreated a Salford street from Victorian times with all the old shop fronts, pubs and houses, simulated gas lamps, shop windows full of the goods of the day (the number of remedies on offer for the relief of constipation were legion) and even 'try your strength' machines. When I first discovered that recreated street (it is housed in the former main library on The Crescent alongside the University, by the way) you had to buy an 'old penny' from the doorman to operate the machine. On my last visit I discovered they had converted the machine to take decimal coinage and it costs a ten new pence piece just to grip the thing —it's not the same is it? Another thing I noticed in that Victorian Street was a post box with the following collection times: 8-30a.m., 10-30a.m., 12-30p.m., 2-30p.m., 3-30p.m., 5-30p.m., 7-30p.m., 8-30p.m., AND 10p.m. plus a collection on Sundays at 8-30p.m. How about that for a service? I wish our present postal service could match even part of that. I live about two miles from the town centre and am often lucky if the post arrives by 3-00p.m. and they seem to have cancelled Mondays altogether!

So I offer that source of inspiration for my prospective film maker — and I hope one will come along and do justice to the classic 'Love on the Dole' — and in return all that I ask, if he has any money left in his budget, is that he remakes 'The Cure for Love' as well. I fondly remember that film with Robert Donat and Dora Bryan in the leading roles. Some of the lines will never leave me, such as Dora, in her biting Lancashire accent, emerging disshevelled from some canoodling in an Anderson air raid shelter with 'a chap' to confront the newly returned Sgt. Jack Hardacre — her putative boy friend — with the words, 'Three years and faithful I've been Jack Hardacre, three years and faithful'. Jack meanwhile throws his weight about regularly telling all and sundry that he's 'Sergeant Jack Hardacre, not some Civvy Street reserved occupationist'. Great film and well worth the effort to remake it.

Mind you the critics in my film guide say that Hobson's Choice was 'brilliantly played' but felt 'The Cure for Love' was an 'antediluvian regional farce' while 'Love on the Dole' they described as 'an old fashioned social drama'. They may have been right at the time but perhaps next time around my hypothetical producer will 'try harder'.

Oh, and one final word, if readers don't know what the cure for love is you find out from some cackling old harridan as the film ends — it's marriage!

Chapter Twelve

It's Them Five Again

We've all done it. We've all tied two door knockers together, pulled the string and run like the devil round the corner to watch the outcome as two irate householders confront each other across the street and blame each other for the disturbance — strange how they never caught on, unless, that is, one of the original perpetrators got a fit of the giggles and gave the game away.

We've all pushed penny bangers through letter boxes and run round the corner once more. No fits of the giggles this time, though. The consequences of penny banger misdemeanours were worse than anything our young minds could imagine.

The trouble was that on our estate everyone knew it was us — the gang of five, that is — and retribution was usually swift. The other trouble was that other, slightly younger, miscreants soon cottoned on to the fact that if anything went wrong we would be blamed and that caused us a lot of grief, not only in being blamed for something we didn't do but in time wasted finding the original sinners and giving them a good seeing to.

In those 30s and 40s it was common to see young lads walking along holding their collars. They'd seen a funeral and the rule was that you held your collar until you saw someone in black. We were lucky in that we had a lot of nuns around then. Nowadays you often can't tell the nuns from the average woman in the street they look so 'modern' and usually they are dressed in grey or blue. If kids still play that collar holding game I wonder who they set their sights on for relief.

And then if you 'trod on a nick, you'd marry a brick and a bee would come to your wedding'. Again the sight of dozens of little lads carefully treading the pavements heads down avoiding nicks in the paving stones was a common sight.

I've said before that our pranks weren't too dangerous or vicious as are some of the things children do today. We didn't beat up old ladies. We did errands for them instead (usually in the hope of getting a 'penny for going'). We, rightly, expected a clip around the ear if we were cheeky. We WERE cheeky but we knew the consequences. We did respect authority, reluctantly in some cases, and we did enjoy ourselves without too much bother to the rest of the community.

One of our pastimes just after the war was to start at nightfall at a given point on our estate and attempt to go through every garden in a circuitous route to get back to the start point without being discovered.

Can you imagine five or six young bloods even thinking they were going to be successful. It was dark, the gardens were irregular, the fences were high and low, of barbed wire in some cases and dustbins always seemed to be in the most unlikely places. And as for the dogs — it seemed we had one for every three households and they knew their 'trade'. We never made it.

However we tried and got the rough end of many a tongue for our troubles.

And then there were the dens we made. We made them EVERYWHERE. In old air raid shelters, out of tied up lengths of grass in the playing field, inside the boiler house of the school, in the blitzed remains of a local shop (we once turned on a gas tap there and lit it. The resulting flames beat anything the earlier falling bombs had created and we made ourselves very, very, scarce), in a discarded school boiler that was gently rusting away in a field, up trees, in garden sheds, in the local builder's yard — that was a good spot — and in the middle of rhododendron bushes. You name it we had a den there,

Of course they were often discovered by rivals and wrecked but that was part of growing up. You did unto them what they did unto you and many a bloodied nose was the result.

Those dens were terrific and in many cases highly sophisticated — in our eyes that is. Carpets on the floor no less — discarded moth eaten specimens maybe, but carpets. Refreshments in the way of cocoa and sugar mixed in a twist of paper and fluff riddled sweets from grimy pockets and light by way of candles in jam jars or old cocoa tins with holes punched in them to give an eerie atmosphere — they also doubled as hand warmers.

Cunning also played a part and we had one den in the school cellars. To get access meant a surreptitious trip to the last cellar of three during the school day to slide open a bolt — try doing that

with a caretaker of the likes of ours. Success meant that in the evening you pushed open a trap door and presto you had a warm, dry, snug and fairly soundproof den.

Another school den was made in the boiler room. This, again, meant making sure a certain bolt which held the coke hole door was left off. Come the night and down the coke chute we went and into a warm glowing den. The unfortunate part about that den was that if someone had to answer a 'call of nature' it became custom and practice to seek relief against the hot boiler sides. The ensuing 'pong' was guaranteed to cause a quicker evacuation than anything the German army ever managed. It beggars description.

The strange thing was that we never invited girls into these dens. I'm talking about us being about 13 or 14 at this time. Girls did play a big part in our thoughts at that age but there was no way they were ever going to be invited into our private domains — rather like gentlemen's clubs I suppose. There was a time and place for girls and the nights when we indulged in crafty smokes and tall tales was not one of them.

Girls were to have their day, but not quite yet. We were more concerned with other things. Like communication, we had some futile and primitive efforts at communication when young.

We read in boy's magazines about creating a primitive sort of telephone system by stretching a string taut between two positions and tying tin cans to the end to act as talk/hear devices. I don't know what we got wrong, but they never worked. Perhaps it was because my friend and I had to stretch the line over the rooftop of a house that stood between ours. We did that by tying the string to a tennis ball and throwing it over the roof when the neighbours were out. I don't think they ever noticed it was there!

We tried signalling with mirrors in true Baden Powell fashion but that didn't work either. Not that much sun in mucky Lancashire in those days — it often gave up the unequal struggle against the smoke and grime — and anyway neither of us knew morse code so it was all pretty pointless — and frustrating as well sitting in the bedroom window signalling like mad without any response only to find your friend had been out all morning.

We yodelled a lot, Tarzan fashion, to attract attention and we left each other notes under stones and then forgot which stones they were under — we would never have made spies. But mostly our means of communication would be by timidly knocking on the friends' door (always the back one) and asking if so and so was coming out to play. Mother's were always at home then and you faced a thorough inquisition about your intentions before being allowed to join forces.

When it was wet we tossed up as to whose house we would play in, always assuming the mother was in a good mood and let us in at all, and then we would stay for hours playing with toy soldiers (most of the time being spent rejoining their heads to their bodies with spent matchstalks the Swan Vesta sticks were the best for that), trains, making balsa wood models, chalking top tops with fancy patterns that would look great when they were spinning, building towers out of playing cards, reading the backs of the cigarette card collections and reading endless comics. Isn't it strange how other children's toys always seemed better than your own?

I even had one friend whose family couldn't run to bedside cabinets for the children. He had an orange box with a curtain over the front. I pestered for ages, without success, for my mother to let me have one of those instead of the proper cabinet I did have.

That same friend had a younger sister who was forever 'hanging on to our coat-tails' and threatening to tell her mother if she wasn't allowed to come with us. 'Go home face-ache' was the normal admonition. That would send her packing only for her to re-appear some time later with the message 'Mam says she wants you home.' We all knew what that meant — we wouldn't see him again that day!

And if we weren't being pestered by younger children we always seemed to be being chased. We weren't bad kids, just mischievous and inquisitive as children are at that age, but that curiosity always seemed to get us in trouble from teachers, policemen, park-keepers, farmers, gardeners from 'the big house' and, of course, neighbours. I've run some miles in my time getting away from stern figures waving big sticks.

One of the nicer things in the early winter evenings was to visit one of the local nightwatchmen. You never had to go far to find one because just about every bit of road works or house building site had a watchman to tend the paraffin filled warning lamps (nowadays they are all flashing battery operated things which seem to spend most of their time on their sides or barely offering a glimmer — progress!) The watchman always had a blazing fire in a brazier with a blackened kettle on top and a mass of grubby mugs in his hut. They always seemed to use 'Cow' condensed milk for their brews — a sweet and thick mixture that probably had no connection with cows or dairies — I might be maligning the stuff because whatever was in it it had a lovely flavour. If you were lucky you got a brew and if you were even luckier you would be allowed to roast a potato on the fire. The blackened object that was finally rescued from the heat looked pretty revolting but the taste was delicious once you had broken through the hard shell.

Chatting about watchmen has reminded me of one incident which even I, as a child, found totally astonishing. During the war all the railings in the park near me were taken away for the war effort but for some reason the gates remained. All that was left of the perimeter was a stone wall about three feet high which was easily climbed. Nevertheless at 8 p.m. every evening the park-keeper would do his rounds blowing his whistle to tell lovers and children the park was closing AND THEN LOCK THE GATES!

Park-keepers were another breed. It seemed as though no matter how far away you thought you were from authority when doing something slightly nefarious a whistle would blow and there would be the 'parky' bustling across the grass (it said not to walk on it but he was allowed to!) It depended on his age and mobility how long we lingered before scarpering.

Not just park keepers but people in authority seemed different in that era.

No traffic wardens then, thank goodness, but we did have some impressive policemen. I remember the one who controlled the traffic at the junction of Corporation St and Withy Grove in Manchester right outside the newspaper offices of the then Kemsley empire.

As a young boy I used to visit my grandmother who was a cleaner at the then District Bank (later Natwest but goodness knows what now) which was in part of the Kemsley House buildings. I was allowed to go into the vaults and recall being able to stand at one doorway and see round two corners into the next passage by means of some carefully positioned mirrors.

When I got tired for wandering around the empty bank (save for the cleaners that is) I would stand in the window and watch that policeman. He always had the same duties and was famous throughout the city. Anyway he was adept at controlling the vehicles and horse drawn carts. A little twitch of the wrist here, a nod there and he kept everything going like clockwork.

At a given time every day a whistle would blow and down into Withy Grove would sweep dozens of two-wheeled horse drawn carts loaded with newspapers for the stations — we had four in Manchester then — and at the same time dozens of little urchins would scatter in all directions with bundles of papers for the city centre news-vendors. On hearing that whistle my policeman would raise both arms, stop all the traffic and let the newscarts through — what a sight that was particularly when they mingled with the same contraptions coming out of the Evening News building in Cross St.

We used to have to queue down a back street to enter our local cinema on a Saturday afternoon and I recall passing the time watching a one man and a boy blacksmiths that was still operating then right in the middle of town. Fascinating to watch the smoke rising from the hooves as the hot shoes were applied — fascinating for a townie that is.

Eventually the back door of the cinema would open and the queue of ragamuffins would rush down the passage to the pay booth. Not many people could control that unruly bunch but one man could. I remember there was this little fellow who was not the size of twopennorth of copper and he wore a jacket that was about four sizes too large for him, but by heck we did as he said. He didn't just tell us to keep in line as we queued to pay — he cuffed us into line.

Then once inside and with the lights down we would start crawling under the seats to reach the dearer ones which meant you didn't have neck ache for a week from being too near the 'silver screen'. We got away with it sometimes as long as we didn't try to be too cheeky and aim for the 'tanner' section, but most times the little fellow would come bustling along shining his torch along the rows and, depending on his dyspepsia I think, either made us go back to our cheap seats or threw us out altogether.

Bus guards were another uniformed lot who could give you a rough time. You kept quiet and behaved or you were thrown off. No arguments.

It's funny how a uniform or other symbol of authority brings out the worst in some people. I remember the air raid wardens with their little tin hats who really did savour being able to shout 'put that light out' and the special constables who delighted in blowing their whistles.

Withy Grove and the horses ready for another edition.

Chapter Thirteen

Walking & Walks

As you walk around today you see coach loads of schoolchildren being 'bussed' to the baths — not so in my day.

Our school was a good mile and a half from the baths and we walked there and back in a crocodile. Obviously you could not get there and back, have a swim and change all in one period so a trip to the baths was at least a two period job and often also resulted in the maths or English master waiting forlornly in his classroom to teach a class that was still making its way back from an afternoon's swim (Amazing how you can procrastinate when you know what waits at the other end).

Those baths at Swinton have been knocked down now but they gave me a lot of pleasure after the initial shock which everyone endured of being pushed in, 'dunked' by somebody leaping on your back from the side or clobbered by someone leaping in from the diving board without looking who was underneath. The real 'hard cases' would change quickly and race upstairs to jump in from the balcony. If you got caught that was you out of the water for the session but it was worth the risk.

We shared cubicles as we changed and that was always good for a laugh as underdeveloped parts were exposed to ridicule particularly after they had been in the water! We showered and went through a pool of disinfectant to make sure our grubby little feet did not offend the baths superintendant — grand title that. Then we wallowed around in fairly futile fashion — too many children for too few teachers ever to have a decent chance of learning.

And that was another thing. Everything was done, if you like, 'from the touchline' because this was wartime and the teachers were either retired men teachers coming back or women. No way were they going to expose their feeble bodies to the water so they 'coached' from the side and pretty ineffective it was too.

But later when the war ended younger male teachers came back and at last we got some proper sports tuition.

Now my school concentrated on Rugby League — definitely a 'man's game' and we were lucky in that one of the teachers who came back from the war was Tommy Watkinson. I didn't know it at the time but he was a top class referee and was devoted to the sport. What that man taught me about Rugby League football has stayed with me to this day. When I became a junior reporter and later reported League matches I would often see Tommy — still refereeing. He would give me a knowing look, grin and say:' Why did you leave the game lad, you could have been a professional.' I don't know whether his judgment was right but I like to think so.

We seemed to spend a good part of our school week walking.

Again we had a mile trek to our playing fields, we had no showers and so after a muddy, rain soaked session on the playing field we would trudge back to school, change into our outdoor clothes, though still with the mud clinging to us, and make our way home hoping all the time that mother had remembered it was sports day and had got the fire going to create some hot water for a bath.

It doesn't really bear thinking about, no school showers and a mile walk there and back for a game. But the thing was we ENJOYED it. Probably because we didn't know things could be better.

Tommy Watkinson got our school involved in football matches against other towns (with an evening newspaper putting up the sponsorhsip for a shield) and for two seasons I played full-back for that team. What a thrill. There was one other school in town playing Rugby League and that was St. Mary's, a Roman Catholic school. We were the best, though, and St Mary's only ever managed to get one player in the side of 13 — the rest came from my school.

But the real thrill was in playing our inter-town matches on the local professional team's ground at Station Road in Swinton. Imagine changing in the dressing rooms of your Saturday heroes and coming out of the tunnel in the town's colours to

the cheers of the girls you had carefully made sure knew there was a match on and that you were playing. Heady stuff.

It seemed that children were forever marching in my young days. We had the Whit Walks, we had the Rose Queen processions, we had the Boys Brigade marching to church on Sunday mornings, we had those huge Armistice Day services and parades (remember how people and vehicles EVERYWHERE used to stop for two minutes silence then) and, if that was not enough, it was common to see little lads marching very stiffly behind squads of Territorial Army soldiers trying, fruitlessly, to keep in step and match the men's strides.

I can't remember which 'lot' (the Protestants or the Catholics) marched on Monday and which on Friday during the Whit Week processions of witness in Manchester and Salford but in my own town of Swinton people used to refer to 'Whisunday Thursday'. They meant Whit Thursday when the 'other denominations' had their day — hence 'Whisunday Thursday' As I say I am not totally sure of the sequence in Manchester and Salford but I remember that if it rained on the Friday one group would remark that 'God looks after his own' and if it rained on the Monday the other group would say the same thing. Strange thing religion.

But those walks were events in those days. The whole town turned out to watch the walkers who assembled all over the town in their churches and chapels and, by a miracle of co-ordination, managed to meet up at approximately the right time for the grand 'walk' through the town centre passing the civic and church dignitaries only to then break off at appropriate points to go back to their start points thus letting the traffic, which had been virtually at a standstill for hours, get back to normal. I .don't think such walks would be possible now given the traffic hold-ups that would be caused.

I said they met up at approximately the right time because it was not easy to get those long columns to the right place on time given that doting parents and relatives would constantly dash from the pavements to thrust coins into the hands of the, sometimes reluctant, walkers. Other hold ups were caused by calls of nature from little excited folk whose parents would knock at the door of the nearest house begging the use of 'the toilet' and by those gushing parents dashing into the procession to straighten Edith's dress or slick down Jimmy's hair with a 'lick and a spit' if the earlier applied Brylcreem failed to do its job.

The Whit Walks were THE events in my town. We had Church of England, Catholics, Methodists (with a host of prefixes), Unitarians, Salvation Army, you name it we had them, all doing their thing. One of the big marshalling points was a croft (now a car park) off Station Road where the columns would be tightly squeezed in to form up for the great march. Bands were brought from all over the place and were in great demand. Besses o' th' Barn, Fodens, Fairey Aviation, the Co-op and colliery combinations, all had bands available, but at a price. Most of the little towns had to settle for their own Salvation Army and Boys Brigade units blowing lustily because the bigger and more well known bands only took part in the big parades in Manchester and Salford.

Now that's a thought. Manchester on Whit Monday and Whit Friday was clogged with marchers from every part — we even had masses of 'overseas' marchers, Ukrainians and Poles etc. So big were those events all the streets were closed in the city centre and the Manchester Evening News and Manchester Evening Chronicle used to use acres of newsprint in producing special pictorial supplements of the event. It is a very pointed indication of how religion has declined that the walks hardly get a mention these days and, certainly, are not considered worthy of a special supplement.

Mind you the same thing applies to the University Rag Week. They still go on but with far less impact than of old. I remember the centre of Manchester being a somewhat intimidating place in Rag Week with hoards of students, outrageously dressed, pressing for funds (rather like time share salesmen pester now) and invading offices and shops and other workplaces in their efforts to raise cash for charities and who stopped the city with their procession — with a big predominence of scantily glad girls revealing acres of thigh above stocking tops. I suppose the feminists have put a stop to that — but it's the charities that suffer.

During the war we had other 'events'. We 'Dug for Victory', we had air force heroes in our midst who urged us to buy aeroplanes (or parts of them) and sailors who beseeched us to adopt a ship. Can you imagine anything less heroic than an aeroplane named 'Borough of Swinton and Pendlebury'? There used to be a plaque on the wall in Swinton Town Hall saying which ship the town had adopted. I can't remember which it was now and now that the town has been absorbed into Salford it may well be that the plaque has gone. I

wonder. I can't honestly remember the Army asking us to adopt a regiment (or even a platoon) but they may have done.

But going back to those Whit Walks. Just picture the scene with hundreds and hundreds of children, carefully chaperoned by sometimes distraught Sunday School teachers, all in their finery and sometimes tearful, with banners fluttering and applauding relatives lining the pavements waving flags and sticks with paper streamers attached sold by enterprising traders who walked the route with baskets of the goods over their shoulders. Bands played, mayors and councilllors waved and saluted and there was mass hymn singing. Great days, gone, I think, for ever.

I did take part in a Whit Walk once — and only once. My mother rigged me out in one of those sailor suits so popular at the time (but not with the wearers). I hated it and hated even more being called 'cissy' by my non-churchgoing friends.

I joined the boys brigade for the uniform — remember the white 'sam browns', the forage caps and the ready availability of bugles for anybody who had enough 'puff' to wring out a note — but I didn't last long. I didn't last long in the cubs either. I joined a group who used to meet on the top floor of Manchester Road Methodist Sunday school. I got as far as my dib dib dubs and sitting round in a circle listening to Akela but after only a couple of weeks I had a fight with another lad and pushed him down the stairs. I had to hand in my woggle and neckerchief after that and I never joined another group until the Government made me when I was 18 and the Royal Air Force were given the task of knocking me into some sort of disciplined shape.

Chapter Fourteen

Big School Days

I have been putting off the leap into a later period when I went to senior school because I had so many memories to recall about my very early childhood. But I can put it off no longer and must move ahead.

It was a difficult thing to leave junior school where I had been in the 'top class' with the rest of the gang and had ruled the roost. When we went to senior school — Cromwell Road Secondary Modern it was called in those days although now they give schools fancy titles such as 'High School' — we were the new kids and had to know our place.

At that time there were two secondary schools in Swinton. There was mine, the tough school, and there was Moorside where the 'softies' went. They played soccer and we played Rugby League — I give the game its rightful capital letters. If you weren't 'thick' you went instead to Eccles Grammar School. The eleven-plus decided all that and I have no objections about selection at that time. I was a mathematical idiot — and still am — but I could put the odd sentence together. That, however, didn't count — you had to be good all round to get a place at the grammar school. Suffice it to say that by haunting night schools and libraries later I made up for the short-comings of my secondary education.

Although we were now at senior school we still had to report home after school on the dot to make sure all was well. After that we could 'play out' to our heart's content until the evening meal. Now to get home to 'report on the dot' and yet still buck the system called for some ingenuity.

For instance now we were at senior school we were a lot further away from home and that meant a bus ride. That also meant bus fares. I lived three stops — long ones mind you — from the bus terminus opposite the town hall and after a little while I worked out that if I ran home and IF enough people got on and off the bus I could beat it to my stop and thus save a penny.

In those days I promise you there was so little traffic you could hear the bus leaving the terminus and so increase your pace all the while praying that there would be people at each stop.

The only problem was the long gap betwcen the stop at the market place and my stop. With the best will in the world and with the best lungs any runner could have you never were able to beat the bus to that stop. The beauty was that the stop was about 50 yards beyond the top of our road so we gained there.

Luck couldn't last forever, though, and there was the occasion when my mother was on the bus I should have been on and saw me puffing and panting at intervals as I passed the bus and the bus passed me, Questions were asked and I could not give a satisfactory explanation and so I was admonished always to take the bus in future. I promised I would. but I didn't keep the promise because the penny saved meant such a great deal.

It meant being able to go into Jones's — a shop that sold all sorts of pressed meats and home baked breads but, more particularly, hot barmcakes. The thrill was to buy a penny barmcake red hot from the oven and break the crust to pull out the hot dough while leaving the main part of the crust intact. The crust was actually the delicacy and like all children we saved the best till last. The difficulty was that you had to do this while running to keep ahead of the bus to 'report on the dot' How our stomachs stood those rigours I don't know but they did and we enjoyed every hot mouthful.

Obviously we couldn't buck the system everytime and had to catch the bus sometimes and obviously too many hot barmcakes palled. Our ploy then was to build up the saved coinage and wait until Friday afternoons when often there would be a late 'free period' which allowed us to leave earlier than normal. On these occasions we would buy a penny barmcake, steaming hot, but this time have it cut in half and laced with butter — a halfpenny more for that. We would then actually amble home well ahead of the bus, save our digestions, enjoy a treat and avoid recriminations about being late home from school. Oh the wiles and subterfuges of children.

Two reports recently caused me to cast my mind back to school days — and particularly senior schooldays.

The first concerned an erudite report about discipline (or lack of it) in modern day schools and the second was about a survey of library facilities in a Lancashire school area where, in one instance, the investigators found an atlas dated from 1912 and a mass of startling statistics about the pausity of withdrawals.

Some time ago I went back to school — only for an afternoon thank goodness — but the experience was a shock to the system.

For a start the language of the children in the playground would have made a sergeant major blush (I think). I had heard, but not experienced it first hand, about the problems passengers faced when 'caught' on the same bus as children leaving school at the end of the day. Someone remarked to me that it took the same degree of bravery as that exhibited at the Alamo. Another said Saturday night 'chucking out' time in the old days had nothing on it. Having heard the playground obscenities I think I know what they mean. If they do that in school goodness knows what they get up to on the buses.

The other thing that struck me was the number of children apparently wandering about with no particular purpose during lesson times. In my day anyone, but anyone, seen walking the corridors during lesson times faced an inquisition from not one but several teachers as they passed the classroom windows. The fact that they were exhibiting all the signs of imminent sickness or urgent calls of nature seemed to matter little.

And the final thing that struck me when I eventually found the classroom I was seeking was the amount of noise. I suppose the most diligent of pupils can cope with all that background muttering and movement — I hope so — because I know I couldn't and in those circumstances education would have been totally impossible. Silence rules — that was the motto.

One thing it did make me realise is that there is no way I could ever become a teacher. I belong to the old fashioned clip around the ear period, and do not make any excuses for believing discipline would be a lot better if those circumstances still prevailed. I can trot out the 'it never did me any harm' argument with the best of them AND believe it AND be totally unswayed by counter arguments. It worked for my generation and it would work again — the only difference now is that it would take rather more time and, probably, rather more instances of punishment. I happen to believe, however, that the long term benefits would be worth it. Swearing at teachers was unheard of in my day and even 'dumb insolence' merited a trip to the head master's study.

We had a teacher called Mr Ashton I remember, although we always called him Drak (behind his back of course) and he had a penchant for throwing blackboard erasers at recalcitrant children. His aim was not too good but it never seemed to matter. If he hit the wrong pupil then he 'owed you one' on the basis that everyone in the class would deserve to feel the thud of the eraser at some time during the week. People of my generation will remember those erasers. They were not a damp cloth or anything so fragile. No it was a wooden backed implement about the size of a clothes brush — only heavier.

Chalk was another favoured missile only that didn't hurt it just grabbed your attention and the cane was commonplace. The teachers would do their own caning for the most part but for the really serious cases it was a trip to the headmaster's study where the really heavy 'artillery' was kept.

After trips to the study you always lingered a while to get the tears to subside and to get your face composed into a suitably nonchalant appearance. It never worked, though, the tear stains were a dead giveaway and anyway everyone in the class had had the same experience, several times, and were not fooled by the 'it didn't hurt me' expression.

In my senior school days I eventually became the school librarian. Now that sounds rather grand. It wasn't. The 'library' was housed in a cupboard in a corridor opposite the cloakrooms. It was open for one hour each day and had a total of about 200 books.

I remember a secret being passed on to me by my predecessor. As long as you didn't try it on too often it was possible to 'accidentally' tip the library cards out of their box just as afternoon lessons were due to start. A variation was to say some lout had done it deliberately. A quick visit to the head's study with sorrow written all over your face usually meant you missed the next lesson in order to tidy up the mess. Needless to say I passed on the tip to my successor.

But the real thrill of being librarian was that every Friday afternoon during the last period you were allowed to go to the central library with about a dozen books for replacement. Being able to have a dozen books of your own choice on a Friday which didn't have to make their appearance in the 'library' until Monday lunchtime was total bliss. All weekend to read (pre-television days remember) and be quite happy to hear your mother say to a friend 'He always has his head stuck in a book'. There can't be much wrong with that sort of criticism and my thirst for knowledge at that time was so strong that I think I might even have fancied that 1912 atlas!

Chapter Fifteen

Holidays — Good and Bad

I have been casting my mind back to some of the 'holidays' — I use the word advisedly — that I have had over the years.

Mind you I have had some memorable and delightful holidays as we all have — but I have had some disasters as well.

I recall during the early part of the war going with my family to Deganwy to stay at a boarding house — Mrs Overton's on Station Road it was — for the usual week's break. Now during the war trains were few and far between for such destinations and you took what you could get.

The only way we could get to Deganwy was by train from Manchester to Llandudno Junction, a train that got us to the junction at two in the morning with no train available to Deganwy until eight am.

The distance between the two points cannot be more than four miles but there were no buses or taxis and our only recourse was to stay on the train as it was shunted into a siding and sleep in the compartment. Mother took one bench seat, father the other and I was put in the luggage rack!

What a start to a holiday. And things didn't get much better because I remember climbing up Castle Hill behind the town and finding a sheep stuck on a ledge. I ran all the way back down to tell my father only to be told to go back up and tell the farmer. I did find a farm, but it wasn't the right one and the farmer didn't seem to be too interested in the fate of a stranded sheep. I couldn't find

another farm so I went back to the ledge. The sheep and I gazed at each other for an eternity before finally it gave up the game and with a quick scramble reached safety and left me feeling more than a little foolish.

If you travel by train to Llandudno and other North Wales resorts you will be confronted for much of the way by lines and lines of caravans. 'Mobile homes' they call them, now though anything less mobile I have yet to see, some of them haven't moved in years. Why do people want to spend a holiday on a strip of land between the railway line and the main road? For that matter why do people seem to enjoy a picnic in a lay-bye — but they do.

Well I ask the question because I did the same thing once — and only once. My family were going down to Cornwall and I didn't want to go. I was a teenager and wanted to 'do my own thing' as they say now although I think it has since changed to wanting to 'find myself'. So I hired a caravan on a site between Conway (or Conwy as they spell it now) and Bangor. Now either the Devil planned that location or someone decided that there is one born every minute and I was one of them because the site had to be seen to be believed- perhaps sight would have been preferable to site.

It was a thin wedge of rather ancient caravans between the main road and the railway line and the caravan I was landed with was right alongside the road AND right alongside the only entrance/exit to the site. The site was also slightly lower than the road so that every time a car left it was revved like mad to make the incline.

I have never been so miserable in my life. I was alone, I could barely cook and so essentially I lived out of tins and I daren't go back home early and lose face.

During the war we had stayed at home holidays with government sent concert parties in the park bandstands and idiotic 'uncles' organising games no one wanted to play. Great fun they were I'm sure.

But every so often you would manage a day trip to Blackpool or, if you weren't fussy about seeing the sea, Southport. I have been there many times and have yet to see the tide in. Mind you the Lord Street shops make up for that short-coming. But Blackpool was the mecca, a crowded train, a walk from the station to the 'prom', an ice cream from Pablo's, a walk along one of the piers, a few rides on the Pleasure Beach attractions and then back to an even more crowded train. Great days.

I must have caught the day trip habit because when I was courting I managed to save enough to buy a Francis Barnett 197cc motor cycle. What scope that brought. Day trips everywhere in the North were now possible.

On one famous occasion I took my wife to be on the pillion — pillion, a piece of foam over the rear mudguard — for a trip to Llandudno. About 90 miles there, a quick spurt round the Great Orme and then a 90 miles trip back. The only thing was I did it all without stopping once! When my passenger got off she walked like a cowboy after a month on the trail.

On another occasion I went up to the Lake District for yet another solitary holiday. I was going to camp out for the first time ever and so I bought an ex-American Army pup tent. The Lake District weather was true to form. I put up my tent in the rain, it leaked like a sieve, everything, including me, got wet through and so in the dark I sought out the farmer and begged the use of his barn, I slept with the owls and mice — wet, but warm.

I couldn't get any of the things dry after that so I had to resort to a bed and breakfast establishment for the rest of the week. The trouble was I hadn't budgetted for that and so the motor bike had to stay unused until I was ready to return home and I walked everywhere. On reflection that was no bad thing because the beauties of the Lakes, particularly Hawkshead where I was staying, are best enjoyed on foot.

As a child I used to love Blackpool, what child raised in Lancashire didn't?, but now I can only stand the place out of season when the 'lights' are over and the summer 'trippers' haven't put in an appearance.

There is nothing finer than a walk along the promenade, particularly at North Shore out of season. The trams still run and give out that famous 'toot' that 'children' like myself will always associate with the resort during the annual Wakes week holiday, the air is usually bracing with a strong wind coming off the Irish Sea, 'Kiss me Quick' hats and rock and candy floss are absent and generally at that time Blackpool is a wonderfully relaxing place for an old fogey like myself to enjoy. But in season, well...

Last summer I had to go to Blackpool right in the middle of the season for a business engagement and any illusions I might have held about its possibilities as a holiday venue for me disappeared instantly. Certainly childhood memories were destroyed.

For a start everything, but everything, was electronic — even the bingo cards. As I walked along the 'prom' I was greeted virtually at every step by the calls of 'She was sweet' and the response 'Sixteen', 'Doctor's favourite' 'Number 9' 'Two fat ladies' 'Eighty eight' and so on. The inanity of it all was overwhelming and yet people were actually ENJOYING taking part in those, seemingly, never ending bingo games at,

seemingly, every amusement arcade — and there are plenty — along the Golden Mile.

But that wasn't the thing that disappointed me most. What I missed were the slot machines of my childhood. Those 'Alluwin' machines where you used to flick a steel ball around the casing aiming to lodge it in a slot at the top — the further in it landed the more money you won, or tried to win, there was a big difference. The rotating trays full of tawdry prizes which had arms with rounded ends you 'controlled' to try to push your choice down a chute and into your waiting arms. The cranes with the grabs which you timed to lower on

One of our holiday haunts was this converted railway carriage based at Coalport in Shropshire. That's me — the little one on the steps.

the prize of your choice as it moved round and the tantalising way the object always dropped from the claws just as it reached your chute — everything was stacked against winning but we unsophisticates still enjoyed the challenge.

I remember the Pleasure Beach where one of our favourite games was to try to get a 'monkey' up a pole by rolling balls into holes faster than the other contestants. 'You're racing now' the man used to say and the excitment was intense.

Then there were the fairgrounds which came round once a year, usually at Wakes Week, when all the mills and pits closed together so families could go on holiday together or stay at home and enjoy the travelling fair while father decorated the kitchen.

I remember that the local newspapers used to send reporters to Blackpool, Llandudno and Rhyl to seek out holidaymakers and find out how they were enjoying themselves. Pictures were taken for the next week's issue when the holidaymakers would have returned and be keen to see their picture 'in the local rag'. It was small world time all the time on those occasions because often you would find yourself in 'digs' next door to your next door neighbour from home. It wasn't really a coincidence because people went back to the same landlady time after time once they found the beds were clean and a food 'ample'.

Anyway to get back to the amusements. At the travelling fairs (ours was usually Silcocks and filled Swinton Market Place one week and later in the year moved to Pendlebury Market where there was much more space). At those fairs you would roll your hard won pennies down a wooden chute and hope they would land — without touching the lines — on a given square which had a winning amount written on it. Invariably they mostly only offered even odds but there were the tempting £1 squares right at the back and in a corner where it was virtually impossible to direct your coin and, anyway, arguments with the stallholder about whether the coin was 'cleanly in' or touching a line took strong nerve, particularly if you were only little and he had his 'mates' close by.

We threw wooden balls — very light wooden balls — at very heavy coconuts and rarely won one, we threw rather blunt darts at cards fixed on rather hard boards and, again, rarely won and we fired rifles at moving metal ducks and could never come to grips with the fact that although we aimed straight the missiles always seemed to go left or right — amazing what a little bend in a rifle sight can achieve!

But now you go to an amusement arcade, a pub, a leisure centre or what you will and you are assailed by whines, whizzes, screeches, simulated machine gun noises faster than any known machine gun could ever fire bullets, pings, pongs and kapows as the computer controlled 'games' are activated. It might excite the younger generation but it does nothing for me. I still like to remember trying to pit my wits on a fairground rolling my pennies down chutes with the sound of the steam organ on the roundabouts behind me and the prospect of a toffee apple on the way home in front of me. It beats space invaders

The games may have been crooked and the odds stacked against winning — aren't they even more so with computer orientated games? — but the sounds were friendlier and the pace less frenetic. 'You're racing now' — I'll never forget it.

Chapter Sixteen

Very Unhygienic

Being ill as a child was horrible. Now I know that being ill at any time is not pleasant but being a child and ill in the 30s and 40s was far worse than anything children suffer today.

For a start hygiene wasn't on top of anyone's list of priorities and if one child in a class caught something you could guarantee the rest did as well. We ran the gamut from nits — mechanical dandruff we called it then — to whooping cough and measles. Now if anyone asks me 'Did you ever have such and such as a child?'' I always answer 'Yes' in the sure and certain knowledge that I did!

The classroom desks were packed close together so the germs had a field day. Bathing was only indulged in once a week- if felt necessary in some households I could mention — and clothing, socks particularly, had to (allegedly) be capable of standing up in a corner on their own before washing was felt necessary.

So schools were a pretty easy breeding ground for ailments. It was the 'cures' that were so awful. Syrup of Figs (if you hadn't 'been') was acceptable, school milk (to build strong bones) was a bit 'cissie' but tolerated, cod liver oil and malt was not bad but horrific without the malt and some cough mixtures were actually quite tasty. But there were horrors as well.

Name me a child of that period who enjoyed Fenning's Fever Cure, Sanderson's Throat Specific. Sulphur tablets, hot lint poultices on festering cuts (cuts always seemed to fester and fathers always applied the hot lint soothingly saying 'It isn't going to hurt' — liars.

There were a host of family remedies for 'what ailed you' then. Doctors were expensive and people did their best to solve the problem themselves. I remember camphorated oil being heated in the oven to be rubbed on troublesome chests, soap and sugar poultices being put on cuts that went 'septic', Thermogene pads being placed on 'weak' chests at the start of winter and not being removed until the spring, goose grease on chests — that ponged at close quarters — and plasters galore. No self respecting lad went around without at least one plaster on knee or elbow and you were really cock of the walk if you could sport a finger stall made from the finger of an old leather glove and tied to your wrist with bandage.

As you recovered being ill often felt quite good. The fever had gone, the spots were disappearing and you felt almost at one with the world — particularly as you couldn't go back to school until the quarantine period was over. You lay in bed with extra plumped up pillows, the counterpane was covered in comics and adventure books and life wasn't all that bad.

Then came the doctor! Now in those days doctors, and teachers, were like gods to our parents. They were on a plane above us and were to be treated with the deference they felt they deserved. What a difference today.

When the doctor was to make a visit (paid for on the insurance or 'on the drip' to the 'Doctor's Man' who called like the rent man, no NHS in those days, the house was in turmoil and the patient was in imminent danger of suffering a setback. For a start before the doctor arrived the bedclothes and pyjamas had to be changed (I have a sneaking feeling those pyjamas were kept solely for the visits and then whipped off the patient and put back into storage immediately afterwards), the window was opened to 'air' the room no matter what the temperature outside or the temperature suffered by the patient, the patient had to totter, literally in some cases, to the bathroom to clean his teeth and suffer a rub down all over with a face cloth and I even know of one person who actually dusted the stair treads before the arrival of the doctor.

There would be an inspection of the patient with a stethoscope and (always) cold hands and then a prescription would be recommened along with further 'bed rest' The doctor would leave with the patient hearing subservient mutterings of 'Yes Doctor', 'Yes Doctor' but never being able to hear what was actually being said about his condition and fearing the worst.

I remember that the doctor's car (always instantly recognisable in the street) was inevitably followed by the visit of a 'concerned' neighbour asking about the condition of the patient. If the visit was accompanied by the offering of a home made rice pudding or egg custard then it wasn't too bad — you could put up with the prying.

In these enlightened times you can be in and out of hospital in a day for minor operations — if you can get in at all that is — then (providing your Hospital Saturday Fund subscriptions, or whatever, were up to date) everything necessitated at least two weeks in a hospital bed and, if at home, a week in bed and then at least a week of convalescence — on a light diet of soft boiled eggs and milk puddings etc. We must have been naive not to realise how much each 'consultation' meant to a doctor then.

The doctor would make up the prescription in his own dispensary and some unfortunate relative (usually father on his way home from work) would call at the surgery for it. The medicine was invariably placed on the waiting room mantelpiece and the doctor would send his 'account' at a later stage — trusting souls they were in those straitened times, sometimes too trusting.

How things have changed. I had reason to need a doctor for something quite minor recently and called on the group practice — doctors didn't even have locums never mind group practices in my young days. I failed, as usual, to get past the gaulieter on reception and on asking for my particular doctor (you get comfortable with the same one don't you?) was told that I would have to wait until the following Thursday to see him. This was on the Friday!. I reflected that the medicine might have been awful but the service was a lot better when I was young.

I went to a family funeral recently and met relatives I had not seen in seven years. I met friends I had not seen in ten!

This started me thinking about the close knit communities of my childhood and of how families lived within a few streets of each other and, thus, retained family ties and built up relationships which, sadly, are no longer possible today with job availability and transferability, the availability of cars and the need to move where the work is.

When I was a child and a teenager the work was on your doorstep. It didn't seem to matter what your job was there was a factory, an office or a warehouse 'just around the corner' with work for you. In those days working for a bank or in the council offices was the height of ambition and those settling for warehouse work were deemed to be in 'dead end' jobs with no prospects. Mind you

His weakness gives him **STRENGTH**

YES, the children have a very decided weakness for "Ovaltine" Rusks. Gratify this weakness, mother, for "Ovaltine" Rusks are a splendid strength-giver, especially if a cup of delicious "Ovaltine" Tonic Food Beverage is taken with them.

'OVALTINE' Rusks

APPETISING DIGESTIVE & NOURISHING

Sold by all Chemists in 1/6 & 2/6 tins.

A cup of "Ovaltine" with a few "Ovaltine" Rusks forms a complete and highly nourishing meal. R.3

those dead end jobs always seemed to pay far more than some of us got as trainees and apprentices and it was a big wrench to take a poorly paid job 'with prospects' when other lads were throwing their money around on lasses.

Families were often close because of necessity. In my case my great grandfather was the only member of the family with a house with a bathroom. All his children, apart from one, (he became a teacher and moved away to 'better himself') lived within about four streets of great grandfather's centrally situated house. There were constant calls for the use of the bath and eventually a rota was drawn up with Billy's family having use of the place on Monday, Cissie's family on Tuesday, Harry's Wednesday, Albert's Thursday and Minnie's on Friday. (It was a good job he didn't have any more children!) Obviously the weekend was reserved for great grandmother and great grandfather.

But that hygienic necessity had another purpose. It kept the patriach of the family in touch with his offspring and their offspring and created a tight knit disciplined (and that's the important point) unit which was able to help each element as the need arose.

Of course not everyone had the chance of using a relative's washing facilities and had to resort to other ways of getting clean. Now I have an old tin bath in my garden which I use as a fish pond — it provides a great talking point — but once they were functional and necessary. Those baths had to be filled from buckets and pans and took an age to fill. No wonder whole families used the same water. There is a joke now when someone says: 'I have a bath every month whether I need one or not'. In the days before bathrooms became standard in most houses that was no joke.

The other alternative was to go to the council swimming baths and use their 'slipper bath' facilities. For a few pence you could buy a bathtub of hot water, rent a towel and come out as fresh as a daisy. I never asked, and so never knew, why they were called 'slipper' baths but every town had them — and well used they were.

Another thing that I noticed recently was that a private firm was refurbishing some of the deck access flats in Salford which had been vandalised beyond the council's ability to repair them. This enterprising firm bought the derelict buildings, redesigned the access points, refurbished the interiors and sold them to the 'upwardly mobile' of the Greater Manchester area as very, very desirable residences.

Now when those flats were built they were, in the words of the slum dwellers who took them over, 'palaces' compared with the insanitary two up and two down rotting and mouldering houses they had been living in.

The question to be asked is why did the residents destroy their environment to such an extent that the council gave up? I don't want to go into the realm of well reasoned arguments put forward by socially aware people as to why vandalism is rife in these places and why grafitti seems to be so necessary. That is for another place. All I would do is point to one or two cases which prove another side of the argument.

Go to New York or Paris or Berlin, in fact most places, and if what we blithely refer to as 'high rise' developments are privately owned they are cared for and acceptable ways of living. Why, if you rehouse former slum dwellers in those virtually self same places do they destroy their environment? Old people live alone in private developments safely. Why are council owned housing units so different?

Why is it that blocks with walkways used by all the residents are vandal free and grafitti free if privately owned and yet are an offence to sight and sound when rented?

Going back to the slums of Manchester and Salford I accept that everything was at street level and more closely watched but people, with very few exceptions (and they were usually brought into line by the disdainful looks of fellow street dwellers) helped each other, nipped potential vandalism in the bud and watched over each others' interests (a sort of early Neighbourhood Watch scheme I suppose).

You could tell which houses in the street had 'class' by the ornaments in the windows and their curtains. I recall the better houses had 'Alice' dolls or plaster models of sweet little boys holding a couple of cherries made from wax — artistically cretinous but pleasing to the residents. Gracie Fields aspidistras were everywhere and lace curtains were a 'must' for respectability. Donkey stoned steps were also de rigeur and any householder who didn't 'stone' the step AND brush the pavement in front of her house was 'no better than she ought to be'. Mind you I sometimes wonder whether all that cleaning plus the washing of windows — which seemed a constant occupation in those smoky old days — was not simply to have a 'nosey' and see what a neighbour was up to.

Life seemed to revolve around household

conversations about what 'her at number ten' was up to and how 'her at number eight' was always late in putting out her washing (always strung across the street) on a Monday. You could tell how people lived by that washing and many a 'disgraced' woman would spend many days drying her washing on a clothes horse (or maiden as they called them) round a fire rather that have the neighbours look at her family's threadbare clothing, scrupulously clean though it may have been.

Mind you don't ever believe that those places were crime free. We've always had rogues and the myth that you could leave your front door safely unlocked while you went to the corner shop was disproved by my grandmother on one occasion. She went to the corner shop and later found £40 missing fron her sideboard. A sizeable amount in those days. So much for myths.

Chapter Seventeen

3d or 6d

I wonder if you remember Woolworths with their offer that everything in the store was either 3d or 6d (old money that is).

My favourite 'Woolies' was the one in Piccadilly in the heart of Manchester. Sadly it is gone now after a disastrous fire some years ago which cost a lot of lives.

But when I was young it was like a honeypot. You could buy toy soldiers in ones and twos in those days from counters with glass sided trays. They stocked the 'boxed sets' as well but if you wanted to replace a battered bandsman and rifleman who had lost his head or base (the most common disasters) you could buy the item singly. It was a great way to get a host of drummers or machine-gunners. I used to like those 'kiltie' drummers, much more colourful than the ordinary guards bandsmen. If you were really plush you could buy howitzers, tanks and other military vehicles.

But it wasn't only toy soldiers you could buy there. It took patience, mind, with only limited funds available, but you could build up a whole zoo of animals and cages one at a time or a farm yard with animals sties, cowsheds and fences. The model pigs were best for me, the chickens were so small they were too fiddly to be bothered with and anyway didn't appear to give value for money — no pigs were best.

My 'Woolies' had a great cafeteria on the top floor where you could take a tray and chose any item of food that was on offer. What a challenge to a small child. Then you would hunt around the huge eating area to find a vacant table invariably having to clear it yourself of the trays and dirty plates left by previous diners The food was basic but it was cheap and that was vitally important in those days.

Toys and sweets were the only things that interested me about 'Woolies' and, in fact, the only things that interested me about shopping at all at that time. I had to be dragged kicking and screaming to buy clothes and standing in "the ladies department" while mother looked at dresses was total agony.

There was another magical store in Manchester at that time and that was Wiles' which stood on the opposite side of Lewis's arcade. (I never got really interested in Lewis's — it didn't have the same magic as the other stores). Now Wiles' sold nothing (at least I never noticed other goods) but toys and games. Imagine three floors, counting the basement (and that was the best department) full of childhood delights.

But it was not just the toys that were the fascination. Wiles was, I think, the only store in Manchester at that time to have those overhead cash containers which whizzed from a central point to the serving point carrying handwritten sales chits one way and change the other. It was worth buying something just for the fun of watching those containers whizz to and fro. It was even more fun to stand and watch near the collection point as the containers came zooming in from all directions just like trains at a huge junction — at least you could stand there awhile until a floor-walker moved you on if you didn't have the required paper bag in your hand as proof that you had bought something.

Even in those far off days Wiles' was a "discreet" store with the serving ladies in black dresses with white collars and everything was quiet and subdued — no piped music thankfully.

They stocked the most fabulous toy trains — electric — and had an irresistible display in the basement just at the bottom of the stairs — how well planned! — and, as you can imagine, it was a magnet for small boys. Not just the trains but every kind of accessory you could think of was available from tunnels to ticket collectors.

But we were blessed with two other great toy shops in Manchester — Bassett and Lowke which catered more for the enthusiast who wanted real steam operated engines and Tyldesley and Holbrook in Deansgate who also did a good trade in trains but specialised in sportswear.

Just about every child in Manchester must have bought his first cricket bat from Tyldesley and Holbrook and his first football jersey and pair of boots — remember those boots? — weighed a ton and had studs that were positively lethal with protruding nails. They needed about a ton of dubbin after every game as well!

I read now of the fabulous prices being paid for the types of toys I have described. Oh if only we could look into the future. Mind you they gave hours of endless fun those trains as you deliberately derailed them into the path of marching ranks of "lead" soldiers. You can't have everything.

I went 'walkabout' in my new 'home town' of Macclesfield recently and, as in the days of old, found myself pressing my (not so grubby nowadays) nose against a toy and model shop window.

The thing that fascinated me most was the miniaturisation of the 'toy' trains. I put inverted commas around 'toy' being well aware that to enthusiasts they are far from being toys. To me that's how I remember them though.

As a lad I remember my first train set was a wind up version with an engine and two trucks which ran round and round a circle of about three foot diameter. That got pretty boring and didn't last long. Neither was it added to.

The next stage was a Hornby gauge 'O' set with a Royal Scot engine, three coaches and a set of trucks (although it seemed infra dig to allow a "Scot" class engine to pull freight). I DID enlarge that set.

First I got a station, then a passe partout tunnel, a few points and a few station staff and passengers and some Dinky cars and delivery vehicles. Put a load of farm animals alongside and behold you had something that would keep a young child happy for hours on end.

Next my father screwed all the rails onto boards (four of them) into an acceptable 'layout'. Having done that it meant that one was doomed forever to the same train routes (although it was fun to be in total control from a console in the middle which you reached by crawling under the boards).

I bought my son a Hornby '00' gauge layout when I felt the need to renew my childhood passion for model railways. That was never quite the same as the majestic Gauge '0' set though — too small and fiddly I thought. I mean when the whole train left the rails, which was often, it never had the same thudding impact as a Gauge '0' Scot train did. If the Scot train fell to the floor (total disaster) rather than just leaving the rails (minor disaster) it was always guaranteed to bring mother or father scurring up the stairs in case there were broken bones.

But now when I looked at that model shop window and saw how small the trains of today can be I was disappointed. I realise that by being small it means you can get more in a smaller space but they all looked so insubstantial and didn't appear to have any chance at all of staying on the rails I suppose they do — but I bet it's only a bump rather than a resounding thud when they leave the rails and hit the floor after a monumental crash.

I know I always used to indulge in monumental crashes on the last circuit before I shut down the layout for the night. Great fun to 'wind-up' the controls so that the train took the bend at an impossibe speed and careered off the rails and into the lorries and farm animals.

One of my friends had an American layout with a multi-wheeled and multi-appendaged engine (typically American). It used to whistle 'whoo, whoo' like the engines do in the Western movies and I used to 'allow' him to put in on my track, It wasn't anywhere near as impressive as my 'Royal Scot' engine and if we contrived crashes on the bends my train always came off best — I think!

But playing with model trains was for rainy

days and winter days. At other times we made our own kites out of two bamboo canes, sheets from newspapers and lots and lots of paste made from flour and water. I remember there used to be a Jewish gentleman who had a loft in the alley behind our house in Salford and he made his living there by unraveling, sorting and selling lengths of string and rope. He always looked fairly ragged and unshaven so I don't think he made much of a living, but there he was and with a bit of cajoling he would 'sell' children short lengths of string (probably because he couldn't get rid of them anywhere else) for us to tie together to make control strings for our kites. Sometimes it seemed there were more knots than string and the time it took to make a worthwhile length was interminable. Still we had nothing else to do, so we did it.

We also had peashooters made from the central spools of cotton reels cadged from the local mills and 'spud' (potato) guns which we bought at huge (to us) cost. We never managed to make a workable spud gun ourselves though we were adept at making a 'gun' which would shoot the cardboard tops from milk bottles (pre silver foil you know).

Catapults were standard weapons and nearly always carried in back pockets and we also spent hours and hours whittling blocks of wood to make model aeroplanes (always fighters because they only had one engine and were easier to make). Some of the lucky ones also had aluminium model planes made as 'foreigners' by fathers who worked in the wartime factories. I still have a model of a 'Defiant' made from scrap aluminium. It probably started life as some housewife's kitchen saucepan which she had loyally donated to the war effort at the behest of Lord Beaverbrook (Minister of Aircraft Production at that time). I wonder how people would have felt if they knew to what use their precious war effort donations were being put?

Balsa wood, when you could afford it, made smashing model planes and ships (this was pre 'kit' days when you used your imagination) and it was amazing what hours of fun a child could have then with a pile of matchboxes and some cardboard and (of course) the required flour and water paste. Stick them all together making (almost) round wheels from the cardboard and presto you had a train that stayed intact for all of three minutes. It was the fun of creating and repairing the things that was the attraction I think. The ships we made always seemed to capsize in the bath as well, we could never seem to get the centre of gravity right

And of course if you REALLY had time on your hands pooling resources to buy a pomegranate and picking the seeds out of your slice and eating them provided hours of endless fun. No problem about the pin to pick out the seeds — no self-respecting boy every went without a pin stuck in his lapel!

With all the discussion about out of town shopping cities and shopping developments. It has prompted me to one or two thoughts, the first being that we are overshopped in many towns and cities now and another is that nobody ever seems able just to open a row of shops. Today, we have to have fancy titles such as 'centre,' precinct', 'mall', 'court', 'exchange', 'experience' and a myriad other gobbledegook names for simple shops. In my day that's what you had — shops with only the Co-op offering any building of decent size and all the big stores kept in the city centres where they belonged.

And frankly I can't recall not being able to find the things I wanted. Admittedly the choice was not as varied as today but if you wanted it and persevered, then you could find it.

I recall a wonderful ironmogery in Swinton where you could buy everything imaginable for household repairs and cleaning. You had to ask, mind you, because when you went in you were so overwhelmed by the mass of goods you couldn't find anything yourself. Nothing was pre-packed in unopenable bubble packs like we get today but I must admit the brown paper bags the purchases were placed in had a tendency to burst on sight. If they didn't, mind you, we kids would do it by blowing into them and frightening the life out of the cat. You wanted nails — 'How many pound'? was the response. You wanted screws — the same response. No one had to buy a pack of ten screws when you only wanted four. If four was your desire then four you could buy. I often used to go there and buy items I didn't really need just for the fun of going and enjoying the smell of the place (paraffin, creosote and polishes all mingled in one magnificent aroma) and trying to catch the shopkeeper out. I never made it but I'll bet when he died the shop died with him because no one else would ever find anything in that magic place.

Then there were those shops — mostly selling fresh food — who white-washed their prices for the day on the window and prayed it didn't rain or else the handiwork streaked. Some of those shop keepers were quite artistic, too, (or was it the errand boy in his spare time) with exclamation marks by the dozen and little wiggly underlinings for emphasis.

Every so often a trip to 'town', Manchester in my case, was called for to buy items unobtainable locally and that was always a treat. The books and records were more up to date, the food choice greater and the clothes and shoes cheaper. But often those trips were used to buy something really special or to get something repaired that needed a specialist.

Now Manchester is totally dominated by an abomination called the Arndale Centre (known locally as the biggest public lavatory in Europe because of it's tiled exterior). Then that area was littered with tiny one man businesses in Shudehill, Withy Grove, and there were hundreds of others in the areas off Oldham Street and Lever Street, all around Chethams school and Victoria Station, down London Road and Stevenson Square. Tailors, watch repairers, gunsmiths, second hand clothes dealers (they flourished), pet shop owners, second hand books dealers, leather goods merchants, toy shops, specialist food shops, haberdashers you name it Manchester had it — and it was all in a jumble. We didn't have 'garment districts' like New York (although the excellent and abundant Jewish tailoring establishments did seem to congregate around Cheetham Hill and Lever Street) or jewellery districts like Hatton Garden -everything was in one great and glorious hotchpotch — and it was fun to find things.

Naturally there were always arguments in families as to which shops had the best value goods and there was always one no-all when you showed him your purchase who could always have got it cheaper somewhere else.

Now all that is gone and if you want something repaired either it is prohibitively expensive or 'there's no call for that' and you have to buy new. If we'd had to buy new everytime in my young days we would have all gone around naked and shoeless!

You could make a smashing day of shopping in Manchester then with lunch (or dinner as it was known in that part of the world) on offer at Woolworth's cafeteria, Littlewoods or, if funds were good, to Lewis's restaurant on the top floor where they even had a band (sorry orchestra) playing for afternoon tea. Another thing I remember about Lewis's was the central circle in the middle of the store. There was a ladder fixed to the side of the sheer walls and every year 'Father Christmas' (actually he would have needed to be a well trained steeple-jack to take on the task) would climb from bottom to top to reach his grotto with delighted children lining the rails at every floor. The grottos of those times were justs as grotty as they seem to be today incidentally.

We also had Henry's Bargain Basement — cheaper even than 'Woolies' and in Oldham Street were the cheaper fashion shops and other stores which never actually had the prestige to make it to the main streets. Because they were always cheap they were also always busy and I recall one day walking the crowded pavements with my parents when someone snatched a handbag. The thief ran off to the usual cries with a police sergeant in hot pursuit (there always seemed to be a 'bobby' around when you wanted one then as well). The thief made one fatal mistake. He left the crowd and ran across the road. In a flash the sergeant had aimed his stick (sergeants and inspectors in Manchester always had this synmbol of authority) and brought him down as it tangled with his ankles. We, as they say now, dined out for ages on that story.

It's sad because in addition to the little shops, Manchester centre hasn't even got a Woolworth's now let alone a Henry's Bargain basement — perhaps there is 'no call' for such places in these allegedly affluent times.

And affluence leads me to one final point. Has anyone noticed that not only don't we build common or garden shops anymore we don't build houses either. Look in any estate agent's window or at a 'spec' builder's sign now and what do you see. 'Executive style' (note the style) 'luxury' 'prestige' developements in 'exclusive' and 'sought after' areas. They soon cease to become 'sought after' after the builders have done their worst. Estate agents now 'receive instructions' and just about everything is 'new on the market.' And these 'executive' (are there no ordinary people now) homes are usually placed so close together that you can touch adjoining walls with arms outstretched. They have the cheek to call them 'prestige developments'. Lead me to my 'exclusive, warden serviced, alarm fitted, retirement home'!

My first car — homemade by my Uncle Henry.

Chapter Eighteen

Trams and Trolleys

With the Super tram ready to move through the Manchester streets once again I was thinking about the transport of my childhood.

When we moved to Swinton we didn't have tramcars. They stopped at a place called Irlams 'o'th Height and were run by Salford Corporation. Instead, if we were to go into Manchester we had to take the bus.

But I had a love of those tramcars and would go to great lengths to ride on them. Going to my grandmother's house meant a tramcar ride, so that was always acceptable and I recall waiting on Broad Street in Salford many a time for a tram which had 'Depot' on the destination board. The ride to 'Depot' wasn't long but it did mean a trip down Frederick Road which was long and steep. To get on a 'Depot' tram and manage a seat at the front of the top deck was an unimaginable delight. The trams used to sway and lurch down that hill and always there was the secret hope that it would not pull up in time and transport you away into the depths of Lower Broughton — unscathed of course.

Coming back from Manchester — I've said before we were allowed to do things like that at an early age without fear of harm or hindrance — I would always plump for the tram to 'The Height' as we called it and be quite happy to walk the rest of the way to Swinton. It seemed a long way to little legs but was only about a mile.

But to visit our relatives in Harpurhey meant going by trolley bus and I loved that almost as much as the trams — but not quite. We used to board those silent monsters on Cannon Street and I always remember that for years I wondered who or what was Ben Brierley — the destination name on the front. I only discovered in later years that it was a pub at the terminus. I used to think the fellow must have been very famous to have a bus stop named after him.

I can remember the chaos of Manchester in those days. The trolley buses couldn't manoeuvre too well, being restricted by the overhead wires — I gather the new ones will be able to go 'off wire' and run on batteries for some of the way — and trams, well, if one stopped they all stopped and Market Street and Deansgate, Chapel Street in Salford and many other busy routes would often be jammed with trams all waiting for a points change or another tram on a popular route to load and off-load.

Later on I used to use Lancashire United Transport buses quite a lot and, again, I always aimed to catch one of those which was a little bit different than the rest.

For some reason LUT had several buses which had an upstairs which had the passageway on one side instead of in the middle and all the seats raised slightly above it (the passageway I mean). I think the object was to squeeze in one extra passengers per row because they would accommodate five people instead of the usual four you got on a central aisle vehicle. That was all well and good until you wanted to get off. Try being at the window end of a seat of five and ask four burly miners to shift while you get off!

Downstairs was equally unfortunate if you were unsuspecting because if you sat on the inside underneath the depression caused by the upstairs passage-way then you hit your head with an alarming bump. The warning signs were always at the front and usually totally obscured. We got used to them but unwary strangers often reeled off those buses.

Buses played a big part in life in those days. Everyone could recite chapter and verse about bus timetables and destinations, in fact many an argument was generated in my family about which bus went where and at what time. Hours of endless 'fun' those discussions provided.

I used to go to Greengate Arches to get a bus home from Manchester to Swinton. I had a choice of several in those days and they were proper buses, not the bone-shaking mini-bus contraptions that abound today. No 'Bee-Line' etc then, they were CORPORATION owned and very proper.

We all had favourites. I liked the blue of the Leigh Corporation No 26 — an express which did stop at the top of my road. There was the single deck No 39, another express with limited stops, the No 12 shared by Salford Corporation and Bolton Corporation which went 'round the houses' to Bolton and the circular nos 27 and 28 which went to Eccles via Swinton. Get the wrong one and you had a heck of a long journey home.

There were others and it was always fun to decide which one would get you home quickest. Often you would disdain the No 28 or 19 even though they left five minutes ahead of your choice

because you knew yours was an express and would (hopefully) pass the others usually on the climb out of Pendleton. Half the fun was sitting at the front upstairs and watching the 'opposition' and praying someone would flag it down and you could sail past. There were no prizes for getting you there first — it was just a private game I and others played.

We had buses (double deckers) with an open platform at the back with a rail you could use to either swing on to the bus as it started to move or swing out from so you could leave the bus 'at the run' and get ahead of your friends in the chip shop queue.

I remember that one of my friends had a father who was a conductor (or guard as they were called then) and if we timed it right and got on his bus we had a free ride. (I suppose after all these years Salford Corporation won't worry too much about the lost fares). It used to be fun as kids to get the front seats upstairs so that you would be sitting over the driver's cab and you could pretend you were driving.

We used to have great games adding up the numbers of the tickets, the punched variety with all sorts of words and symbols on them, to get what we regarded as a 'lucky' total. We would collect them (we collected everything in those days) but what we collected them for is beyond my recall.

No 'guards' on buses now — although reading about some of the assaults on bus crews it does seem we are not far from bringing them back — possibly armed — and progress has meant the drivers sitting where they can be attacked by drunks. They need radio alarms and goodness knows what else now. In my childhood the driver sat in splendid isolation in his own cab, with a blind that the guard could pull down to stop the glare from inside in the evenings. The guard would ring once for the bus to stop, twice for it to start and if he rang three times the driver would be out of his cab and round to the back of the bus to help with whatever trouble had occurred — usually an argument about paying the right fare or some such trivia.

Then there were the football buses. Few people had cars in those days and I can remember going to Piccadilly — before the redevelopment of the 'upmarket' bus station — and catching one of the countless buses which followed one after the other to load up with fans for the Maine Road ground of Manchester City. Even my own town of Swinton would have Station Road lined with buses for a big Rugby League match to take the visiting fans back into Manchester.

The old saying: 'There will be another one along in a minute' was true of the bus services of those days. In later years when I used to cycle to work in Urmston via Trafford Park the number of buses taking workers home to their various destinations from 'The Park' were uncountable. And if they were 'bridged' when a vessel wanted to get into Salford Docks along the Ship Canal at rush hour the queues of buses on all the roads around Barton swing bridge — the only access into Trafford Park from the North in those days — was a sight to behold.

But I would willingly lose about half-an-hour on my journey home just to travel by train. There was no reasonably near station to my part of Swinton but that didn't matter. If there was no rush I would 'let the train take the strain'. Doing that meant going to Exchange Station and catching a 'stopper' to Wigan. I didn't go to Wigan but that was the train that stopped at Swinton. I remember now sitting in one of those non-corridor compartments hoping no-one else would come in, and they usually didn't, and waiting for the train to start.

Usually I was so early that I would be sitting there when the steam loco would be coupled to the train with a bump. Another anticipatory wait and then the guard would blow his whistle and you would lean out of the window to see him waving his flag (confirmation that it really was your train that was about to move) and off you would go.

About a mile up the track you stopped at Salford Station (although no-one ever seemed to get on or off there) a little further and it was Pendleton High Level (the Low Level line was to Bury, I think), then Irlams 'o'th Height, Pendlebury

(which was actually nearer my home but meant a shorter rail journey and that wouldn't do) and Swinton. Reluctantly I would leave the train and walk the couple of miles home. I probably could have saved money (in fact I'm sure I could) and done the journey much quicker by bus, but the train had a magic for a child that nothing could replace.

The trains were better then too. None of these dreadful, uncomfortable, and breakdown prone Sprinters that British Rail are wishing on us now. We had 'proper' trains, trains that had a 'rightness' about them. The 'locals' or 'stoppers' were corridor-less. But they still had thick leather straps to pull down the windows and pictures of far away resorts and beauty spots to admire and always, always, a mirror. The expresses had corridors and blinds to pull down at night — just dare to try that now with all the assaults that go on — but we didn't have buffet cars or dining cars. If you wanted food you made a quick dive onto the platform and grabbed a meat pie or sandwich from the refreshment room. The number of trains I have nearly missed and been hauled into as they moved off clutching a meat pie are legion. I can't remember missing one, though, but it could get a bit confusing on Crewe station when a few trains were in and a lot of whistling was going on.

I remember my period of train name spotting and boat name spotting. I suppose every youngster did it, but were they as dedicated as I was?

Does anyone still remember the Ian Allan train spotter books for the LMS, LNER, GWR and Southern Railway? Remember carefully and neatly crossing through the names and numbers of the engines you spotted?

Where I lived in Swinton we were about a mile from the main Manchester line to Bolton, Blackpool and points north. Every night after school I would cycle to the side of the tracks at just 4.50 to wait for the first 'namer' to come through. There was another at 5.00, another at 5.10 and another at 5.20. That was it then, home for tea.

And there were the train trips to Crewe and Derby and Gorton where the LNER locos were serviced (Manchester at that time was essentially an LMS city).

I remember a kindly driver letting me shunt the engine (under very close supervision) out of Patricroft Loco Sheds and a signalman at the box just near Swinton Rugby League ground who let me pull the handles and signal to the box ahead. Magic for a youngster things like that.

And then — as we lived near the East Lancashire Road — there were trips to Golborne where the main Euston-Glasgow line went under the road. Now that was 13 miles away but the trip was often made easier by waiting on your bike for one of the many cotton-bale loaded lorries wending their way to Liverpool. You waited until the lorry went past and then cycled like mad to catch up, cling to one of the ropes and hang on for 13 miles. The drivers never knew you were there — this was in the days before near-side wing mirrors.

The only drawback to all this was that on the way back the lorries were unladen and you couldn't catch them. So you faced a long cycle ride home. Funny how the wind always seemed to be against you on the return trip.

Boat names were another fascination and living fairly close to Salford docks (as we Salford born people insist on calling them, although everyone else seems to favour Manchester Docks) it was fairly simple to peer through the dock gates to get the names of the boats berthed there. I remember No 8 dock always seemed to have the biggest ships.

But Salford docks wasn't big enough for my ambitions and a friend Denis Hinchliffe and I used to cycle to Liverpool, leave the bikes — not lock them — those were the good old days — and climb aboard the overhead railway — the 'dockers umbrella' — and travel up and down the line overlooking that vast complex of docks. What a sight that was. I remember the White Empresses, the Isle of Man packet boats and boats laden with every kind of cargo imaginable. Where has it all gone?

And another thing. Not content with cycling all the way to Liverpool we would often take the 'scenic' route back by cycling through the Mersey Tunnel to Birkenhead and back home via the Cheshire lanes. Try cycling through the Mersey Tunnel these days.

Cars seemed to need a service every five minutes in those days and I remember once going on a trip to Blackpool in a car owned by the father of a friend when the only words spoken, or shouted, were 'kick it'. This was because there was some fuel pipe blockage just under the floor where the front passenger sat and that unfortunate had to stamp on the floor everytime the engine faltered. We got home but it was a worrying journey.

But in my childhood it seemed everything was delivered by horse and cart. In fact thinking back apart from groceries just about everything could be had from a trader with a horse and cart, or even from one pushing his cart himself.

Almost at Salford Docks and a long way from its Far Eastern start.

The 'paraffin man' would come. He sold paraffin for the all important paraffin stoves which augmented the coal fire. But he also sold clothes pegs, clothes lines, home made soaps and detergents (although we didn't call them detergents then). There was the 'pop' man with his array of stone jugs of dandelion and burdock, lemonade, sarsaparilla and ginger beer The greengrocer was a regular caller with his wares stacked at an angle on the sides of the cart. Often the fruit would fall off and we would grab it while he drove on oblivious to the loss. The milk came by horse and cart and was ladled out from big churns into whatever receptacle the housewife offered. When I was still quite young I used to help on the milk round and worked extremely hard just for the pleasure of doing it! I must have been mad. The round took ages and at the end of it I had to walk about a mile home clutching my 'reward' a pint of milk in a jug.

Coal was by horse and cart (much stronger horses for that job) and even the binmen used horses. It was a common sight to see little kids running along the street with a bucket and shovel to get to the horse droppings first. It was good for the roses, you know. I remember once trying to do a good deed for my father walking across a couple of fields to get some cow 'flops'. Unfortunately I used a sack — no plastic bags then — and as it was so heavy I slung it over my shoulder to take it home. The rather gooey mess seeped through the sack and onto my back. I was not very popular with my mother after that episode!

But we had other street people. I distinctly remember men and women knocking on doors to beg and others who would walk the streets singing for pennies. Tuneless they may have been and possibly often the worse for drink but they were also pathetic. I hope we never get back to poverty on that scale when people have to demean themselves so.

Bikes were everywhere in those days. I remember you had street credibility if you had a bike with drop handlebars but one of my favourite bikes was owned by my mother. Mostly the wheel sizes were 26 inch in those days but mother had an old black painted monster with 28 inch wheels AND you had to back-pedal to stop it. It went like a dream down hill but was impossible to ride up even the smallest gradient. I used to go to the grocers on that bike — it had a basket on the front handlebars and another behind the saddle. Downhill all the way there and then I had to push it back up the Manchester Road hill loaded (well not exactly loaded, it was war-time) with groceriees.

Talking about shopping reminds me of how goods were sold in those days. The grocers, in fact all the shops, had chairs for customers to sit on as they waited. And wait they did, on reflection, because the shops were gossip centres and everyone joined in. It took ages to buy your goods then not like the impersonal supermarkets of today. But really were they all that efficient? Shopping was a full time job, what with the queues, the cutting up of 'points' from ration books during the war and the individual weighing and packaging of butter, bacon, cheese etc. (not forgetting loose broken biscuits). It took ages.! I don't think we could afford to go back to those times even though we may hanker for them nostalgically. They were in truth a real pain.

Chapter Nineteen

Save the Cinema

It's all very well signing petitions and making protests about saving the historic buildings but what about the Adelphi Cinema in Swinton?

Mind you that's a futile question because they've already knocked it down. However there are many other cinemas in the region that deserve our efforts.

But that cinema housed and entertained many thousands of people and it was important to them all. They remember Hopalong Cassidy, Flash Gordon, the Three Stooges, Laurel and Hardy and George Formby to name but a few. Not quite as esoteric as Romeo and Juliet I'll grant you but to those people just as important.

The point I'm trying to make is that we lay rather too much importance on saving some historical monuments and artefacts and not on others. Mark my words in a few hundred years historians will be cursing us for destroying our art deco Odeons after having first turned them into Bingo Halls.

Saving scrolls and manuscripts is all very well but who is saving examples of the penny lucky bag, the sherbet dip with the liquorice tube, the toffee apple and the roast chestnut and baked potato ovens. We're making an effort in the case of steam engines and mill looms particularly in the conservation conscious North and we're pretty hot on old canal boats and trams but what about knocker's up poles, donkey stones, black leaded grates, dolly tubs, Valour paraffin stoves, 'Osokool' 'fridges' (I use the word in quotations marks as a mark of respect for the inventor's aspirations), three-wheeled Bond mini cars and the Ian Allen locomotive spotters handbooks (for steam engines that is). Many of those things are of recent memory but they are fast disappearing.

Places like Salford Museum, the Manchester Museum of Science and Technology, the Air and Space Museum (also in Manchester), The Ellesmere Port Boat Museum, Quarry Bank textile museum at Styal in Cheshire, the Macclesfield Silk Heritage Museum and the Crich (in Derbyshire) Tramways Museum are doing their bit but it's an uphill battle.

It's commendable to save ancient monuments, it's commendable to preserve the mini-car (yes, I remember my first one, red and bought in Bolton) and our works of art should be kept in this country and not allowed to be exported abroad.

But I want my Adelphi cinema restored and saved, I want the trams and trolley buses of my childhood restored and put back into working order, I want the memories of horse drawn ice cream and coal carts kept, I want to hear the street cries again and I want my 'den' in the rhododendron bushes, which hid me from so many prying policemen, preserved for all time. It's not too much to ask — is it?

When remembering my father's D.I.Y. exploits I failed to recall the labouring his efforts entailed — and that the labourer was me.

Great Clowes Street, Broughton in 1945, with the front of the Victoria Cinema sticking out on the right.

I seemed to be constantly being told to 'Go to Hamer's yard and bring me a bucket of mortar (or sand as the case may have been).

Now Hamer's builders' yard was only about half a mile from our house but try carrying a bucket of mortar that distance when you are only little. It was a case of changing hands every three or four steps and stopping every dozen or so. It was a good job father wasn't in a hurry!

This was all before the days of owning cars. I did try once balancing the bucket on the saddle of my bike but I couldn't control the handlebars and hold on to the bucket at the same time. Result — disaster. I didn't get a 'penny for going' that time.

Another of father's haunts was a store called Forresters at Irlams-o-th-Height. Now that was a good distance from home and it was a common sight to see father at the front and me (much lower) at the back with lengths of timber between us walking along the East Lancashire Road to home.

When he got the stuff home major construction

work would start and that was usually when I made myself scarce.

When I did I would often go with the gang to our local park. There they had the usual dilapidated swings, swingboats and roundabouts but not much else. I still have a scar on my knee from those days when I got my leg trapped under one of the roundabouts. People were always daring others to swing so high they went over the top. I suppose it was possible but I never saw anyone fool enough to try it — not even us.

We were occasionally successful in luring girls onto the swingboats. It called for a lot of subterfuge and innocent looks to get them to venture on. Two lads would often swing the thing in a gentle fashion all the time offering to give the girls a ride. Once on they'd had it for another four lads would emerge from the bushes and in seconds that thing was banging against its stops at the top of its travel. We only did it to hear them scream because it wasn't a lot of fun for us really — hard work if the truth were known.

But our park didn't have a pond. If you wanted a pond with ducks then you had to venture into Salford to Lightoaks Park. They had a pond there but you couldn't do a lot with it except watch some overfed ducks waddling about. The whole area was surrounded by railings and nosey park keepers. You wouldn't think those places were created for enjoyment the way those 'parkies' used to chivvy us about. A sort of 'You're not here to enjoy yourselves, you lot' attitude seemed to prevail.

Buile Hill park had a big mansion in the middle but that was reserved for full day outings as was the Agecroft Valley. Not far away by car but we walked everywhere and it took some time, especially as we found something fascinating to look at just about every ten yards of the way.

The Agecroft Valley sounds very grand but actually it was an industrial dump but it did have a lot of interesting things in it for kids. There was the grotty canal for a start and a railway where you could while away the time watching the trains run over the half-pennies you had laid on the line. We used to get those coins about three times their original size by putting them under train wheels — if you could find them among the ballast that is. They always seemed to be thrown for miles and, of course, there were always constant arguments about whose coin was whose after the dates became blurs.

Then there was the Chloride battery factory surrounded by high fences and on the other side of the canal and — thus — out of reach. We concocted some very sinister tales about what went on there. Just the smell of the place was enough to fire young imaginations.

Finally there was the point where the rail lines divided, one going to Bolton and the other to Bury at Clifton Junction. That literally was the end of the line for us. No one ever ventured beyond that point and usually we made our weary way home from there stopping at even more interesting sights, every ten yards — of course.

Do children have as many pets now as we used to. I notice lots of dogs around but usually they are being taken for 'walkies' by adults and I understand that gerbils are fashionable — we had never heard of gerbils when I was a lad — but what about white mice, guinea pigs, frogs, newts, sticklebacks and, of course, a little mongrel of

Don the dog which lost its back legs in an argument with a tram. Dad was just about the taller. The picture was taken in Monsall St., Manchester.

your very own?

I have been told, although I was too young to remember it myself, that my father had a huge Alsation dog called Don which was his pride and joy. The trouble was that when I came on the scene Don got jealous and tried to 'go for' me on occasion. Each time it did this father would take it out into the back yard and beat the daylights out of it. Despite the fact that when it stood on its hind legs Don was nearly taller than my father it never retaliated and took its beatings without a murmur.

Whether the beatings would ever have had the desired effect I don't know because not long after I was born Don had a argument with a tramcar and came off worst. The dog dragged itself home without its back legs and died in my father's arms.

We had other Dons after that which I remember well and we also had red setters. But most of all we had mongrels. Bitsas we used to call them — bits of this and bits of that.

I had a succession of them which father bought for me from Tib St in Manchester after much 'mithering' and one in particular called Judy I recall with affection.

That dog knew when any member of the family was coming down the road. It seemed to spend its life with its head poking out of the privet hedge and watching for the first signs of its various masters. From about 200 yards it would spot you, leap off the wall, and race like something possessed to greet you. When you saw Judy coming you dropped everything, school satchels, shopping, everything to be ready to catch the leaping bundle as it bounded into your arms nearly knocking you off your feet. I wonder if we deserve such loyalty from animals?

I used to take piano lessons (didn't we all?) and would take Judy along leaving her outside my tutor's house for an hour while I practised my scales. I recall one winter putting Judy on my sledge, dragging her to the music lesson and then coming out to find her shivering with cold but still sitting on the sledge waiting for me. I was content to drag her back on the sledge after that display of loyalty.

Judy finally had to go when she invaded a neighbour's hen run and saw off several of his chickens. Once they've got the taste, I was told, they'll do it again. So Judy was destroyed but every time I went near that hen run I would snarl and mutter imprecations concerning my hopes for a limited future for the owner — and that his hens would stop laying.

I never invested in a goldfish bowl because the goldfish and other marine creatures which we either caught or bought never lasted long enough for the investment to be worthwhile. Instead I used to use one of my mother's glass fruit bowls often coming downstairs in the morning to find my fish dead by the side of the bowl having managed to leap out.

I did make a lot of rabbit hutches and mouse cages though.

I recall one occasion someone gave me three white mice. I was told they were two males and one female but, being unable to 'sex' white mice at that age, I just looked at them decided the two biggest were the males and put them in a separate compartment from the female. A few weeks later I found out how wrong I had been when the two 'males' presented me with a litter of babies.

That solved the sex problem though, didn't it? I now knew which were the males because it was obvious who was the mother of those babies by all the nuzzling the little ones were doing. So I confidently rearranged the sleeping arrangements and put the two males together. A few weeks later I was proved wrong again when yet another 'male' presented me with a litter of pink nosed babies. What I had were two females and one male plus, now, a mass of 'tinies'.

They were a drug on the market those tinies. No one wanted to take any of them off my hands and they were starting to cost me an arm and a leg in feed and bedding. I finally managed to browbeat a lad younger than myself into taking the whole lot off my hands but he was not that browbeaten that it didn't also cost me all the cages I had carefully built plus a couple of shillings.

We all had pet rabbits as well and it was common to be sitting at home when mother would say 'Whose is that black and white rabbit in the back garden ? 'A quick look and I would say 'Oh that's Wally's. It's got out again, He'll be around soon.' And so it was. Wally would appear to be told his rabbit went 'thataway' and off he would go to search the neighbouring gardens. It wasn't just Wally, of course, we all lost our rabbits from time to time. Perhaps it was because although we became adept at making cages we never managed to manufacture secure locks.

Mind you white mice had their drawbacks. It was no easy task to convince a young girl that she ought to be pledging undying affection to you above all the other lads on the estate when she was transfixed by the sight of a white mouse popping its pink nose out of the breast pocket of your jacket!

Chapter Twenty

Sticky Things

'Sticky' things played a big part in my childhood in the 30s and 40s. One was the Co-op divi checks which were given with every purchase and stuck on 'divi' sheets. It was a form of saving and every so often when 'divi' week came around the housewives would flock to their local Co-operative store to get the cash their checks were valued at. Things were pretty good for a while in the days immediately following the 'divi' payout. Can you remember your 'divi' number.

The Co-op was king in our part of Lancashire supplying just about everything from groceries to coal. They were big employers too with jam works and butter works and insurance offices abounding. They ran a cheap line in funerals as well and it seemed as though every area of town had a Co-op. To be the manager of one of their shops was a mark of esteem in the community.

If you lift your head up now and look closely you will see many of the old Co-op shops have been converted to other retail uses but the name Co-operative Wholesale Society and a date will often still be above the new facade.

Other sticky objects which were so common were flypapers. Every kitchen had one of the sticky traps hanging from the ceiling and it was only replaced when 'full'- and in those days that did not take long with no refrigerators and only 'meat safes' (remember those square boxes with mesh all round to keep out the flies). I was fascinated by those flypapers and would watch the struggling creatures for hours. I used to try keeping a tally of how many were caught but it became pretty near impossible and anyway maths were never my good point.

Now sprays abound everywhere to keep flies and other pests at bay and look what it has cost us in threats to the ozone layer. It's very true that often progress is not necessarily a good thing. After all flypapers worked and they were cheap. I can't say a lot about the hygienic aspect of having a mass of dead flies hanging overhead but has anyone thought where the fly you zap with an aerosol goes too?

Another sticky object which played a big part in my childhood was father's gluepot. Now you buy stuff in tubes which sticks your fingers together. Father had a special pot which had an outer casing to hold water and a smaller central container for the glue which he used to buy like slab toffee and break into lumps. The idea was to put the gluepot either on the gas stove or alongside the fire so that the water would boil and melt the glue. It worked very effectively and was also very effective in causing a mass exodus from the house the smell was so terrible. Once father had applied that stuff to his woodworking efforts nothing on earth could have got the pieces apart — or so it seemed.

Cobbled streets were the norm in those days before we sank under a sea of tarmac and in high summer when the tar between the joints melted little lads would be everywhere gathering the melting tar onto lollipop sticks or bits of firewood and then rolling it into sticky balls. Even our futile imaginations never managed to find a use for the collected material and all it did seem to do was bring parental wrath on our heads as butter or margarine had to be used as a solvent to get the sticky black mess from our hands, faces and (often) hair. Parents were not best pleased with us then and don't forget it was always hot in summer then — wasn't it?

Something else which stuck was black liquorice only in this case it stuck tastily to our teeth. You could buy it shaped like pipes with 'hundreds and thousands' on top to represent the burning 'tobacco', you could get it in the shape of catherine wheels with a tempting hard sweet of varying bright colours in the middle and, best of all, you could get it like shoelaces — long, thin and capable of lasting a long time. We used to call it 'Spanish'.

One final sticky object of the time was chewing gum. Always a favourite with boys who could chew it all day and augment the flavour with 'Spanish' or other sweets or purloin a pinch of sugar to sweeten up the rather tired gum. Beech Nut was the commonest variety but there were posher ones (and costlier of course) like Wrigleys — I seem to remember you got six pieces instead of the five Beech Nut offered. There were some fancy varieties in different colours which were not popular with the lads — maybe they were aiming for the female market — and there were round varieties which were popular as part of the contents of penny 'lucky' bags and also standard fare from machines strategically placed outside newsagents shops.

As usual lads always found ways to do tricks with the gum like blowing it into bubbles and making popping sounds (there was even a variety made specially for that trick called, naturally, bubble gum) and contests would be held to see who could manage to stretch it farthest with one end held between the teeth.

When going into the classroom the favourite storage place for the chewed gum was behind the jacket lapel and that also had dire consequences because on some material such as tweed it stuck the two elements together and could only be prised apart with effort and with an end result which left a sticky mess on the jacket and, yet again, another telling off. The gum was pretty grotty as well containing, as it then did, more than its fair share of bits of material.

There used to be a popular song which went 'Does your chewing gum lose its flavour on the bed post overnight?' It wasn't fantasy that is in fact where it did go until morning, it DID lose it's flavour and it took a lot of chewing to get it pliable again!

What has happened to the firms which used to make the rubber spouts for the (inevitably brown) teapots which (also inevitably) used to have broken spouts.

What has happened to the man who came round the streets on a contraption vaguely resembling a bicycle and, by some mechanical feat of dexterity turned it into an instrument for sharpening household scissors and knives.

What has happened to the makers of cut-throat razors so beloved of barbers for shaving the whiskers off old men and the necks of newly cropped schoolboys. Those cut throat razors were

the weapons of the Glasgow razor gangs which filled our impressionable young minds with dread but were relatively civilized compared with the weapons and antics of gangs today whose sadism is beyond belief.

What has happened to those firms who made the vast quantities of patent medicines which abounded in the 'good old days' those seemingly endless cures for constipation — what was it about our diet that caused such a proliferation of things to 'get things moving', those compounds of bile mixtures, blood mixtures, fever cures, throat specifics, wart removers (what happened to warts by the way?) pastilles for every known throat and chest ailment and other wonder cures that could solve everything from 'screwmatics' to headaches and biliousness. Now people are 'hung over' or 'under the weather'. Then everyone claimed to be 'bilious'.

What happened to the makers of hard boiled sweets compounded of tastes and smells children of today have never experienced. Can you still buy 'winter mixture'? I know I can still get Fishermen's Friends, Victory V Lozenges (although they have been over packaged now), Uncle Joe's Mint Balls (unchanged except for now having a pesky wrapper), Uncle Luke's cough tablets (who's friendly 'uncle's' were those people I wonder) and, probably if I look hard enough, I'll find some Zubes although I'll bet they have been also so repackaged as to be unrecognisable now. The tins Zubes were packed in and the tins of Ovaltine tablets were the 'hold-alls' of many a young lad — particularly for the 'makings' for illicit cigarettes.

But the real jaw breakers were the sweets which came from glass screw topped jars with scents that filled the shop when they were opened. Few shops seem to have unwrapped boiled sweets on offer now. Go into Woolies now and it's all 'pick-and-mix' or else everything if wrapped up to the nth degree so that it takes a mastermind to get through the wrappings and then when you do the product is so bland as to be unrecognisable from the makes of other manufacturers.

What has happened to the makers of Alice dolls and Boy Blue dolls which seemed to decorate every 'parlour' window in those streets of interminable cheek by jowl houses. Are they now making donkeys in hats for Costa del Booze trippers to bring back from rowdy Spain? What happened to the makers of paperweights with lighthouses inside which became snow scenes when shaken or kaliedoscopes which made endless different fascinating patterns from bits of coloured paper when shaken. What has happened to the makers of those detested clay marbles which no self-respecting lad would compete against with the true glass missiles and what has happened to those infuriating metal puzzles every child used to receive at Christmas but never got to play with because the adults always grabbed them and spent hours frustratingly trying to get apart before quietely slipping them between the chair cushions. Mind you there was always some Smart Alec who could do them blindfold.

Where have the spinning top makers gone? The diabolo constructors? The people who made skipping ropes with ball bearings in the handles for easier turning? The makers of yo-yos (although I hear they are making a come back, in a sophisticated form of course) and where are the people who painstakingly put together those 'flick cards' which you held firmly in your fist and flicked to make a semblance of a moving picture sequence?

What has happened to the makers of building bricks with paper print outs of brick blocks, pillared doorways and windows with coloured paper 'glass' in them which offered endless permutations to young constructors? What has happened to the makers of 'sweet shops' which, again, every child seemed to receive at Christmas, with tantalising little jars of varying over sweet confections, little scales to weigh them on and cardboard money to trade with. The only sweets I liked from those collections were the cherry lips.

Where are the people who brought us liquorice roots which we chewed endlessly in the days of sweet rationing (maybe they now supply health food shops), where is the manufacturer of hot potato ovens. The potatoes from them were delicious on a Saturday night liberally laced with rough salt. The ones we tried to bake on our bonfires usually ended up with a 'crust' about an inch thick and a shrivelled and, usually still quite raw, piece of potato in the middle — that is if you could find them in the embers.

What has happened to the people who made the naptha lamps which made market visiting such a magical experience, the pen nib makers (They come as a boon and a blessing to men, the Pickwick, the Owl and the Waverley pen), the people who made the ink to put in those huge stone jars which were a part of every school scene and, in fact, where are the makers of the glazed inkwells we used to have to clean with a bit of rag at the end of every term — it usually took the rest of the term to get the ink stains off our hands!

What has happened to them all, what has happened to childhood. Why can't some things stay the same forever?

The sound of clogs on cobble stones. Instant nostalgia, isn't it. But think about it. Was it such a pleasant sound?

I can remember in Swinton and Pendlebury, just outside Manchester (or was until Salford gobbled it up under local government re-organisation — thank you Mr Heath!), that there were many mills — and all of them working!

You could tell the time by the mill hooters in the morning, at lunchtime and at home time and if that was all the time you needed to know then you had no use of a watch — not that many of us could afford one. If you wanted to know the time when the hooters weren't blowing, then, in the words of the popular song, you 'Asked a Policeman'. And he would tell you as well, instead of telling you to 'Move along now sonny'.

But in the mornings you would be wakened, not to the sound of birds singing but the sounds of those clogs on cobbles and when the mill girls were eventually let out at the end of their shift the air would be filled with raucous shouting. You see, rather like school children at playtime on a windy day, the girls had had to shout above the racket in the weaving sheds and when they were freed they couldn't change their habits. The whole town shared in their gossip!

And if the mill hooters weren't sounding then those at the pits were — and we had four working in the area at that time. Indeed it was a noisy era.

It was a time of home deliveries and of street traders. No infuriating musical chimes on the ice cream vans (or carts as they were then). Instead it was a bell similar to the one that called you to assembly at school and it sounded loud, clear and with regularity — mostly on a Sunday. Then there would be the rag and bone men shouting for trade and offering donkey stones in exchange for old clothing. They were loud, but not as loud as the market traders. Now when I walk through the markets of my adopted home town of Macclesfield — and we have three (there's posh) all the noise comes from the chatter of customers and the shrieks of children — I always avoid the interminable school half-terms when I shop — with the traders just standing around drinking endless cups of tea and waiting for you to ask the price of what you want to buy.

Then it was all 'spiel' by the traders with each one vieing for trade against the other. On Salford Market at Cross Lane — now gone under the weight of a multi-storey block of flats — there was one famous character called Barmy Mick who could outshout the lot. There were others but none compared with Barmy Mick and I could spend hours watching him work. In fact my mother used to leave me watching Barmy Mick while she did the rest of her shopping in the sure knowledge that I wouldn't wander off. Give me a toffee apple and that barmy devil and there was no one more contented.

Other noise came from the tram cars. I am as nostalgic as anyone and am happy to see that Manchester and other towns are reintroducing trams. Sadly they are being modelled on the European versions with single decks and twin cars. They will not be the noisy Leviathans of my childhood which would sway and toot their way around the twin cities of Manchester and Salford. But, let's face it, they were noisy, particularly when they negotiated a points complex and they were uncomfortable, with wooden seats and open front compartments upstairs. Still, they were cheap and you couldn't ignore people and not talk when everyone faced each other in two long lines.

There were steam rail engines with all their accompanying whistles and blowing off of steam and there were lorries but tney were so infrequent that you could actually tell what vehicle was coming up the hill, unseen, by the note of its engine. They were noisy but, as I say, infrequent. Now there is constant traffic noise and it is often accompanied by blaring car radios which must surely lead to deafness problems for the drivers. If I were to be anything other than a journalist I think being a hearing specialist might be profitable in years to come.

I often walk in the Peak District and it seems wherever I go, however quiet it is, I can also hear the distant sound of traffic and that's sad. But it's not as sad as the advent of pile-driving which recently had an impact — not a joke — in Macclesfield. How did the builders of yesteryear go on without pile drivers I wonder? Wren overcame it building St. Paul's and Mr Sunlight did a good job with Manchester's first skyscraper without causing cracks in neighbouring properties. Perhaps it's convenience and speed. Whatever it is I wish it long gone.

Chucking out time at the pubs was an entertainment with those who had imbibed too much treating all and sundry to choruses of Nelly Dean and the wartime favourites. Now chucking out time seems to be linked with rival gangs fighting, drunks kicking in car door panels and throwing anything that moves at passing vehicles. The beer was stronger then so I can only assume, rightly I think, the change has come about by a drop in moral standards.

Every time the wind is in the 'wrong' direction planes fly over my house as they leave Manchester Airport and I swear the noise of one of those second generation jets is far louder than the combined engine notes of the 1,000 bomber raids of the war years and the spread of noise seems so much greater.

One noise I do miss, though, is the sound of a newspaper office with all the reporters banging away at typewriters instead of silent (or almost) word processors and that lovely sound of linotype machines setting the next day's stories reaching an unbearable crescendo as deadline for the first edition approached. If you haven't experienced it then I can't convey the excitement of it. Deadlines are still there, but it's not the same. Maybe in future years when, so they tell me, computers will be voice activated today's generation will look back nostalgically at their first word processors. Somehow I doubt it.

Chapter Twenty One

People and Phrases

My father was a man of stock phrases as were many people who's formative years were the 30s and 40s.

People of those generations, and I include myself, were brought up on musical hall characters and, of course, radio comedies which had, as a necessary part of their format, a host of stock phrases which passed into common usage. Many of us can remember ITMA (It's that man again) with Tommy Handley which had a veritable host of catch phrases. TTFN (Ta ta for now) was probably the most famous but there were others which were used in a variety of circumstances by the man (or woman) in the street.

It's amazing how people can adapt phrases to everyday circumstances. There used to be a duo called the Western Brothers, very laid back and, to working class people, toffee nosed but their catch phrase of "Play the game you cads, play the game" was used in the streets of Manchester and Salford totally out of context, but with a meaning to the people who used it.

There was Sandy Powell with "Can you hear me mother", Frank Randall with "Ee I'll warm thee', Norman Evans with his "Eee did she?" with the requisite adjustment of the bosom "over the garden wall". All these phrases were in common usage in the 30s and 40s along with a host of others from music hall acts such as "Well, let's get on with it", "Let me tell you", "Mind my bike" and "I thank you". Totally innocuous now in cold print but they were 'catch phrases'

and they 'caught on'. I remember people saying their farewells with "Abbasinya" which to them sounded like "I'll be seeing you". That one lasted for years.

But back to my father. If something amazed him he would always "go to the foot of our stairs." Nobody could ever work out the reason for the expression and why it should be said in a voice of amazement, but it was. Another favourite of his was "Never in the memory of man" when he didn't believe something. And if he thought someone was trying to 'con' him, to use modern parlance, he would describe it as "kidology".

A party at home was always referred to as "having a do in a lad's lobby" again I could never understand the connection.

People a little bit simple were "not a full shilling" or "doolalley" and cigarettes, well, what can one say about the names for them.

"Gaspers" was common as was "weeds". Fag, I think, is still used today but what about 'coffin nails' usually applied to Wild Woodbines, just about every young lad's first 'real cigarette' when smoking experiments were indulged in.

I say 'real cigarettes' because being, nearly always, short of cash, we lads would search the gutters looking for fag ends which we collected in tins and then laboriously sorted discarding the paper ends and mixing the variety of tobaccos into some sort of smoking mixture. It sounds pretty disgusting now but we couldn't either afford real cigarettes or be allowed to buy them by shopkeepers and so that was our only source of smoking materials.

The clever ones either obtained a Rizla machine for rolling real looking cigarettes or were adept at rolling cigarettes with their fingers again using Rizla cigarette papers. The cowboys on the films always seemed to manage that with consumate ease but we found it terribly difficult and either lost the tobacco or ended up with something limp and horrible which fell apart at the first puff.

The total idiots settled for hollowed out acorns and straw and made pipes. Two puffs and that was the end of your pipe and you had to start all over again.

When we had been totally hooked on smoking, and in those days just about everybody smoked, we got to the serious bit of obtaining supplies. My heavy smoking period (I stopped about 16 years ago, by the way) was from about 12 upwards and, particularly during the war, it was very nearly impossible to get cigarettes. Later when things eased up a bit after the war you could often get five 'English' cigarettes but had to also buy Turkish offerings called Pasha and Passing Cloud. To English tastes they were pretty abominable but better than nothing I suppose.

There used to be Craven A ('Does not affect your throat' was the slogan) but it was considered 'cissie' to smoke what we called cork tips (now they call them 'filter tips'). The really big smokers settled for Woodbines, Players Medium, Senior Service or Capstan with Capstan Full Strength being reserved for the really hopeless cases. Players Weights were alright if you couldn't get Woodbines but were rather frowned on otherwise and posh stuff like Du Maurier, De Reske and Churchman's No 1 were totally out of court.

American cigarettes were much sought after although in reality they were not a patch on British products. I think it was the glamour of the flip top packets which attracted us, we all felt like Alan Ladd. But in reality anything smokeable in those days of shortage was acceptable. I looked in a kiosk recently and couldn't recognise half the offerings. What happened to Airman, Turf, Strand ('You're never alone with a Strand')?

I walk around one thing that strikes me is how few boys whistle as they go along. There was a time when my relations used to call me 'Whistling Rufus' because I was always walking along (usually with my hands in my pockets) whistling away to my hearts content. Mind you I was not alone. Just about every boy, and particularly delivery boys, whistled and got told off for it by irritated householders. I wonder what they would make of the racket that goes on today.

I was walking in the hills recently and came across an obviously experienced young walker (judging by his expensive rig-out that is) blithely coming along the footpath with headphones on. A fine way to enjoy the countryside that is, I'm sure.

But back to the whistling. Apart from the, often tuneless, renditions of the popular songs of the day, every lad was able to put two fingers in his mouth and produce an ear-piercing note when trying to attract the attention of a friend. This was usually done outside the friend's house as a signal for him to come out to play. It was also usually accompanied by the throwing open of a window by some irate busy-body telling you to 'clear off'. And it wasn't 'words to that effect' either people were more polite then but still got their message across.

Other noises missing today are the sounds of football rattles that people used to take to matches and whirr around incessantly to the gathering annoyance of the purists. The more enterprising lads used to make their own rattles by copying the designs and some of the results were so big it took super-human efforts to get the things to turn at all. The really lucky ones, just after the war, inherited former air raid warden's rattles which had been issued in case the sirens failed and as a warning that gas was about (it never was though). Those were fine 'instruments' and, painted in team colours, were a prized possession.

In those days fans could mix on the terraces, little lads were always passed over the heads of the crowd to sit on the touch line where they could see, people always seemed to be fainting (was that because of poor nutrition I wonder?) and on big match days the roads outside were lined with corporation buses to take the fans home. Very few had cars then and you either walked it if you were local or got a bus if you were a visitor and wanted to get to the city centre. Those buses rocked from side to side as they travelled with the fans upstairs reliving the highlights of the game.

And partisans could shout for their side — often with very amusing repartee — without fear of retaliation. In fact both sides enjoyed the exchanges. Now it's all 'Ere we go, ere we go', 'You'll never walk again' (to the tune of 'You'll never walk alone, the Liverpool 'anthem'). Mindless chanting from mindless people. No wonder they have to be caged in now. But it is a shame.

At that time I used to go to the Swinton Rugby League ground which backed on to the Manchester to Blackpool line. Often a better highlight than the match was standing on the

East Lancashire Road c. 1934-39, Irlams O' Th' Height.

terraces watching the frantic efforts of firemen as they tried to put out a blaze on the railway embankment caused by a passing steam locomotive. Embanknments were always on fire in those days.

But that was not the only problem on the railways. Put your head out of the window and you invariably got a eyeful of burnt cinder and often in the non-corridor local trains of those days the only way to get out of the compartment was to drop down the window on it's huge leather strap and reach the handle on the outside. Many times you would find the window stuck solid and have to go on to the next station which had a platform on the opposite side before you could get out. Try assuring an irate father that that was the truth of the matter when you were late home. Apart from delivery people who brought just about everything to your door then the only other people to knock would be gypsies selling pegs and 'good luck' charms, beggars and Kleeneze salesmen with a ''brush for every conceivable household task''. They used to take your order, you having selected from their samples case, and then deliver the articles a few weeks later. Now every post brings piles of junk mail and many telephone calls are from somebody canvassing for some product or other. I find an answering machine is the answer. Friends soon get used to the dreaded instrument and it does bring peace.

The other thing was pianos. Just about every family who could run to it had a piano then and someone in the family who could play it. I can remember our instrument was an old upright with brass candlesticks on the front and several keys which were either out of tune or wouldn't play at all. That piano demanded a great deal of improvisation. Mother would play 'Lily of Laguna' interminably with the family gathering round joining in the singing (in a variety of keys of course) or else it would be 'In a Persian Market' with everyone singing louder and louder as they got to the chorus of Baksheesh, Baksheesh, Allah. Back to noise you see!

I have been thinking about some of the fishing exploits we used to get up to.

Where I lived we had three working pits (coal mines). There was the Wheatsheaf, the Newtown and the Sandhole. Needless to say they have all gone now.

Now Newtown Colliery at Pendlebury had a 'dam' where water from the pit used to be pumped. It was always warm — even in warm weather you could see steam rising and in the cold weather it was like a fog. That 'dam' had not just got carp in it but GOLDFISH and if you managed to catch one of those you could sell it to the local pet shop on Chorley Road for what was, to us, a sizeable sum.

Needless to say that meant we spent many leisure hours around the 'dam' with home made nets and our hands trying to land a goldfish. The good spots (mostly where the water drained away) were at such a premium that lads had to take it in turns and the time allotted was carefully monitored. We never caught many and the serious fishermen (mostly off-duty miners) were forever chasing us away.

We used to haunt the local golf course as well. There were quite a few ponds on the course but the only safe one — safe in that if the greenkeepers chased you you had a decent chance of escape was the one near the East Lancashire Road. It was the biggest as well but the attraction of some of the more remote ponds was that they contained newts and there were not many places where you could catch those in an industrial town.

My parents were always criticising me for not having enough patience. They should have seen me — and the rest of the gang — around that pond. We would lie for ages on our stomachs with our hands getting more and more wrinkled from the cold water just for the chance of catching a tiddler with our hands — we never ran to fishing rods until later, although we did try (having read the comics) to catch them with a bent pin on a piece of string.

Every so often a lad would leap up (thus spoiling the concentration of all around him) and start frantically looking for the fish he had flung out of the water and into the long grass at the back. We kept them in jam jars — not for long though because they always seemed to be lying belly up the next morning. If you were quick, though, you could swap them for something else before that happened.

The town had dozens of mill 'lodges' as well and they were great places for young fishermen. I recall with two second hand rods a relative had given me (greenheart tips with wooden reels) taking my friend Denis to one of those lodges. He had never fished before, I had used the rods about twice so I was an expert, wasn't I?

We'd been at it all morning without a bite and I was just sitting on the bank with my sandwich packet open when suddenly there was a flurry and a cry of 'I've caught a fish' repeated several times each time at a higher pitch. He had and he landed it right on top of my open sandwich packet! In later years when I took my children fishing in Shropshire, Denis came along as well. My son and daughter and Denis had rods and so did I but I never got my line into the water.

Only he fished the pond and so the fishing was excellent. Now the children and Denis were squeamish and couldn't put the maggots on the hooks. They couldn't take the fish off the hooks either and, as you might imagine, they caught them by the dozen in those under-fished waters. I never stopped taking fish off hooks and putting maggots on all afternoon until I rebelled and took everyone home.

On another occasion we went to Preesall near Fleetwood. I remember that occasion well. Two families had hired caravans near the sea and, because of petrol rationing, we all had to cram into the back of a delivery van one of the party had the use of to get us there. We couldn't have the back doors open because we weren't supposed to be using petrol for that purpose and it was pitched dark. The women relatives sat on deckchairs while the men and children had to sit with their backs to the sides — bum numbing on a 50 mile non-stop journey.

Anyway we got there and Denis and I walked to a local fishing spot and bought licences for the week — we would only have been about 14 at the time. Once again it was a marvellous fishing spot and once again we caught lots of fish — although we had to stay fairly close together because Denis still couldn't take fish off hooks (why he ever bothered to fish I really could never understand).

We had a bait pail with us which would hold about a gallon of water and we crammed all the fish we caught into that and took them back to the caravan. We rustled up an old washing-up bowl and then spent the rest of the holiday watching them die one by one. Ah well!

Chapter Twenty Two

Fifty-a-Side

There are a million incidents any one of us can relate about our school days and probably many of them would be identical — after all many of us grew up in close knit communities where 'customs and practices' were passed on by word of mouth from one street to the next. Little wonder that street games and the words for the various activities were so similar throughout the North.

At my senior school the main playtime pre-occupation was soccer. But not soccer as we see it on television screens with monotonous regularity now. Our 'soccer' was played with a tennis ball with about fifty on each side and with absolutely no finesse whatsoever.

Non-combatants got in the way at their peril and often were dragged into the fray purely by the numbers of other children about them.

With so many children kicking and banging (often at an unseen target) it was little wonder that injuries abounded. Also with so many people taking part it was common for some smart aleck to put his foot over the tennis ball and stand there in an innocent pose while the rest of the mob darted here and there frantically looking for the ball — in many cases they really thought they were chasing the real thing. It took some nerve to do that, though, because the wrath of about 100 hoodwinked kids realising they had been made fools of was not to be taken lightly.

Then there was the bike shed duty. If you were new to the school you were 'allowed' to keep

watch while the older boys had a 'drag' in the sheds. Your reward was a drag — and I mean only one drag — on the sodden end of a cigarette that had been passed around about ten other kids before it got to you.

One of our other occupations was to line up along the edge of our playground and look into the girls' playground. Ours was higher than theirs so we had a grandstand view of their activities — early voyeurism I suppose. That was disrupted with alarming regularity by the duty teacher in the playground — fraternising with the opposite sex was not encouraged although it was impossible to stop with the schools in such close proximity.

We used to hate rainy days in my school. The cloakrooms were caged in affairs where each child had a 'peg' on which to hang personal belongings while in school. If it rained we were forced to sit QUIETLY on the benches in this cloakroom, often among clothes steaming from the early morning rain soaked journey to school. It seemed that just about every time you opened your mouth the duty teacher would tell you to shut up. Oh joy!

I also remember the time I wore my first pair of long trousers (or keks as we called them). I would have been about twelve at the time and the only way I could reach this 'adult' status was to volunteer for the school play. The part I was offered necessitated me playing a country squire — Me! — can you imagine the reception I got at a council secondary school. Anyway to fit the bill I had to wear a dark suit with, obviously, long trousers — who ever heard of a squire in shorts? My father was a tailor and he made the suit for me. Impeccable it was as well and I sailed through the play — despite the catcalls — with flying colours. I also never wore short trousers again after that so it was worth it. Incidentally the only line I had to say in that play is still with me today. 'Of course it is, and to prove it there's his footprint'. Of such things are Thespians made.

One final memory of those schooldays comes to mind. I have written earlier about the return of the teachers who had been in the war. Well one of them, a Mr. Jones, was not used to the customs and practices that had grown up while he was away and he 'butted heads' with 'Drak', our maths and art teacher (every school seemed to have a Drak and Minotaur in those days). We thought our Drak was the epitome of evil at that early age. He lost a deal of credibility, however, when one of the lads found his private hoard of Health and Efficiency Magazine in the stock room.

On this particular occasion Mr Jones stood at the bottom of the steps as we were changing classes shouting 'Keep to the right boys'. Drak at the top was shouting 'Keep to the left boys' The confusion was total to the great delight of the boys who made the most of their discomfiture.

So much for schooldays. Now it was time to start work in the harsh post-war world and all the problems that entailed.

As a young 'sprog' in the Royal Air Force in 1950.

Epilogue

They Say Never Go Back

They say never go back. But to end these childhood memories I decided to revisit my old haunts in Broughton in Salford and Swinton and Pendlebury. I wish I hadn't because by doing so I destroyed a lot of childhood illusions. Better, I think, to keep your memories.

In both places I got lost several times in areas I thought I knew like the back of my hand. In Salford I went down Frederick Road — that veritable mountain of a hill which the trams used to race down to the depot at the bottom. With mature eyes it now looks as though even an old man with a stick would have no difficulty climbing it. The grand red brick depot is still there although now it is some sort of small enterprise centre connected to Salford University.

I went a little further and turned into Broughton Lane. I know it was Broughton Lane because the street sign said so. The trouble was it only lasted about ten yards and then was cut off by a huge fence. By devious means I guessed my way into Great Clowes Street in the heart of Lower Broughton and started to feel slightly 'at home'.

The old Tower Cinema looked forlorn and very, very tired. Closed as a cinema these many years it has had a variety of uses since and the agents' boards told me it seeks yet another owner. The barracks where I used to see the 'Terriers' marching behind the band ever so proudly on Sunday mornings — there's a scout hut there now and the row of shops where I used to press my grubby little face to the window — particularly of Gilberts the toy shop — they have gone. But the Grosvenor Hotel the focal point of the district (I used to run past there because I didn't like the smell of the beer and smoke and the noise the drinkers made) is still there. I wonder if there are still the arguments among families about the amount of money spent in there. I know there used to be in my days and it was common for some housewife to stand outside on a Friday haranguing her drinking husband for not giving her the 'housekeeping' before he started boozing.

The Victoria Cinema at the other end of the street was one of my favourites, it had such grandeur. Someone made a bold attempt some time ago to create a theatre there — it failed and now the dear old building is — yes, a bingo hall.

But the pubs in Lower Broughton Road seemed to be standing in fairly splendid isolation. Some have been 'Watneyised', some have been given fancy new names, but still they stand. Strange how in any redevelopment the pubs stay and the houses go. There are houses roundabout, of course, but they don't nestle alongside the pubs as they used to.

Another thing which struck me forcibly was the smallness of the place. To me as a child it seemed like a whole world of streets with so many houses, shops and pubs that you could get lost in easily. Now it looks as though you could circle the whole area in about 15 minutes.

Both the houses I lived in have, of course, gone. I didn't expect anything else after all these years and with so much redevelopment and Grosvenor Square, the scene of so many happy memories, is almost unrecognisable. Part of it is now called Grosvenor Gardens though anything less like a garden would be hard to find. It still has the railings round the square. Odd that so many other things have disappeared but the railings have stayed.

Everything looked so temporary and cheap. There were few people smiling — there's not a lot to smile at there — and I left saddened that people had to live in such an environment. Lower Broughton was never a pretty place but it deserves more than the planners have given it.

As I started to leave to make my pilgrimage to Swinton and Pendlebury I forgot myself and turned into the other end of Broughton Lane. Of course, that was like the other end — just a short stretch and a fence so I tried again and made it out.

At the edge of Swinton at Irlams o' th' Height I got lost again. The road I had used to often which went alongside Forresters hardware store — like an Aladdin's cave to my father that place was — was not there. I made two other attempts and finally found myself on Manchester Road. I pulled in to look at my old junior school and 'Bamber's Hill' where we tobogganed with such abandon. It looked about 20ft high and with only a shallow slope. Bluebell Hill looked equally small. It didn't seem possible that we had played 'roly poly' down that with seeming danger to life and limb. I bet the children of today can't dig for 'piggy nuts' there as we used to.

Down Barton Road where I spent so much of my childhood and youth. The garage my father built was still there but much else wasn't or had been altered beyond recognition. Great inroads for housing and school buildings had been made into the field where we spent so much time footballing and burning grass and just one tree — the one we always thought was the biggest and best — survived.

The biggest shock I had was when I discovered that the valley — the railway cutting which was the scene of so many battles with the lads on the other side — had been filled in. I stopped to wonder if those 'Valley Gang' lads — the council house lot, as they were called — were really as rough as we made out. Yes, I think they were.

It's funny, you always expect to see faces you knew when you go back to scenes of childhood. You never see one. After all you moved away so there's every reason for them to have done the same.

I went further into Swinton, past the Farmer's Arms with its still dangerous wall protruding into the footpath. They have a beer garden alongside it now but I find it difficult to imagine it attracting many customers situated as it is alongside a very busy road.

I had already gone past the site of the Adelphi Cinema, the venue for so many Saturday afternoon matinees, before I realised it. Once again houses have been built on the site.

Much of the main road to the town centre was recognisable although I was shocked to see the huge 'carbuncle' of an extension to what was once a rather impressive Town Hall.

Most of the middle of the town has been converted into the inevitable shopping precinct with all the inevitable multiples. As they all seem to do it looked pretty soulless.

I thought Swinton Rugby ground was the same until I turned a corner and found one stand had been replaced by a squash club and the Townsend Road stand had gone altogether. Pity, that was a cosy stand only about ten rows deep and you got a knowledgeable class of spectator in there.

Swinton once had a vast moss which was one of the haunts of L S Lowry but more and more houses have infiltrated so that now it is hardly worth the name. Perhaps that's why the sign now reads Moss View Lane (lately Moss Lane). I can't think of any other valid reason for such a seemingly nonsensical change.

There are still plenty of mills to be seen on the sky-line, although not now producing much in the way of cotton goods, but the most prominent, The Acme, which could be seen for miles around has been demolished as has the baths which stood close by.

Things I thought would go on forever have gone. The Ellesmere Cinema — the posh one — has gone to be replaced by a 'Watneyised' pub. I remember my father once won a small amount on the pools and treated all the close family to a meal there. We thought it very much the 'bees knees' at that time. And Critchleys, once one of the premier fashion houses in the entire area, is now Charlie Brown's garage for goodness sake. Swinton is not as depressing as Salford, it never was, but it is bad enough. I shan't go back, I'll stick with my memories.

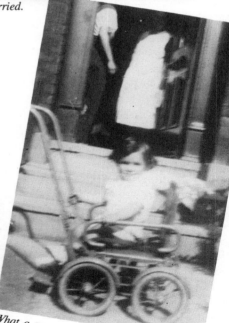

Ken and Margaret shortly after they were married.

Ken outside Grosvenor Square, July 1934.

What a sweet child I was and note the long curly hair.

Four generations. My Grandmother 'Minnie' is on the left, Mum is on the right and my great grandmother is in the centre.

125

Stories and Tales of
Old Merseyside

STORIES AND TALES OF OLD MERSEYSIDE

LIMITED

5

More Stories of
Old Lancashire

If you have enjoyed this book, there are 4 other titles available in the series, all taken from the original 2 Volumes of *Lancashire Stories* By Frank Hird

STORIES & TALES OF OLD MERSEYSIDE

STORIES & TALES OF OLD MANCHESTER

STORIES & TALES OF OLD LANCASHIRE

STORIES OF GREAT LANCASTRIANS

Selected and Edited by
CLIFF HAYES

Stories and Tales of
Old Manchester

STORIES AND TALES OF OLD MANCHESTER

Selected and Edited by
CLIFF HAYES

Stories of Great
Lancastrians

STORIES OF GREAT LANCASTRIANS

Selected and Edited by
CLIFF HAYES

PRINTWISE PUBLICATIONS LIMITED

ISBN 1 872226 21 3

Stories and Tales of
Old Lancashire

Selected and Edited by
CLIFF HAYES

OTHER BOOKS TO LOOK OUT FOR BY
PRINTWISE PUBLICATIONS LIMITED

ILLUSTRATIONS RELATING TO THE HISTORY OF MANCHESTER,
SALFORD AND SURROUNDING DISTRICT ISBN 1 872226 00 0   £2.99

RALSTON'S VIEWS OF THE ANCIENT BUILDINGS OF MANCHESTER (1850)
ISBN 0 904848-06 X   £2.99

PICTURES OF OLDE LIVERPOOL. (Drawings and sketches — Herdman)
ISBN 1 872226 02 7   £2.50

LANCASHIRE HALLS (Margaret G. Chapman). Sketches, photographs and a short history
ISBN 1 872226 03 5   £2.99

MANCHESTER IN EARLY POSTCARDS (Eric Krieger). A pictorial reminiscence.
ISBN 1 872226 04 3   £2.50

CHESHIRE 150 YEARS AGO (F. Graham). Unique collection of 100 prints of Cheshire in early 1800.
ISBN 1 872226 07 8   £4.95

LANCASHIRE 150 YEARS AGO. Over 150 prints reflecting early 19th century Lancashire.
ISBN 1 872226 09 4   £4.95

GREETINGS FROM THE WIRRAL (Catherine Rothwell and Cliff Hayes)
ISBN 1 872226 11 6   £3.95

BRIGHT AND BREEZY BLACKPOOL. (Catherine Rothwell) includes short history of the Tower and the Piers
ISBN 1 872226 13 2   £4.95

SOUTHPORT IN FOCUS. Glimpses of the town's past (Catherine Rothwell)
ISBN 1 872226 15 9   £2.50

PORTS OF THE NORTH WEST (Catherine Rothwell). A pictorial study of the region's maritime heritage
ISBN 1 872226 17 5   £3.95

SUNRISE TO SUNSET (life story of Mary Bertenshaw)
ISBN 1 872226 18 3   £4.95

STORIES AND TALES OF OLD MERSEYSIDE. (Over fifty stories included)
ISBN 1 872226 20 5   £4.95

STORIES AND TALES OF OLD LANCASHIRE (Cliff Hayes)
ISBN 1 872226 21 3   £4.95

STORIES AND TALES OF OLD MANCHESTER (Cliff Hayes)
ISBN 1 872226 22 1   £4.95

STORIES & TALES of OLD MANCHESTER

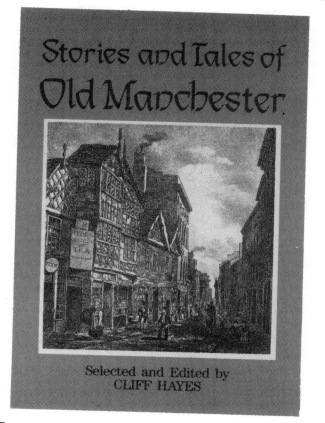

Stories and Tales of **Old Manchester.**

Selected and Edited by
CLIFF HAYES

PUBLISHED BY PRINTWISE PUBLICATIONS LTD. AVAILABLE NOW FROM ALL GOOD BOOK SHOPS. PRICE £4.95